A Book of Irish Verse

A Book of
Irish Verse

Edited by W. B. Yeats

With a new introduction by John Banville

London and New York

First published 1895 by
Methuen & Co.

First published in Routledge Classics 2002
by Routledge
11 New Fetter Lane, London EC4P 4EE
29 West 35th Street, New York, NY 10001

Routledge is an imprint of the Taylor & Francis Group

© 2002 Michael B. Yeats

Introduction © 2002 John Banville

Typeset in Joanna by RefineCatch Limited, Bungay, Suffolk
Printed and bound in Great Britain by
Biddles Ltd, Guildford and King's Lynn

British Library Cataloguing in Publication Data
A catalogue record for this book is available from the British Library

Library of Congress Cataloging in Publication Data
A catalog record for this book has been requested

ISBN 0–415–28982–3 (hbk)
ISBN 0–415–28๐๒ ๑ (hbk)

CONTENTS

Anonymous

INTRODUCTION TO THE
ROUTLEDGE CLASSICS EDITION

William Butler Yeats thrived on dissension. Conflict was his inspiration, as artist and as man, and he was nowhere happier than in the thick of the culture wars. He was thirty when in 1895 he published *A Book of Irish Verse*, 'towards the end of a long indignant argument,' as he wrote in the preface to the second edition in 1900, an argument carried on 'between a few writers of our new movement, who judged Irish literature by literary standards, and a number of people, a few of whom were writers, who judged it by its patriotism and by its political effect.' Hardly a new dispute—one as old, indeed, as Plato—yet momentous not only for what was to be the future of Irish literature, but even for the future of Irish life in general.

In the 1890s, after the death of Parnell and the political vacuum left by that event, Yeats faced the dilemma of deciding which kind of Ireland he wished to promote. From early on he had understood that his poetry would be inextricably linked with the destiny of his country. He had spent much of his youth and young manhood in London, and it was there that he had his most vivid life. Ireland, however, was a constant call to 'the deep heart's core,' as he wrote in his early poem, 'The Lake Isle of Innisfree,' the inspiration for which, according to his *Autobiographies*, was a glimpse of a miniature fountain in a London shop window. When he was in Ireland, the choice was between Dublin's drawing rooms and committee rooms, where the din of nationalist wrangling could deafen an ear as finely tuned as his, and the woods and shadowy waters of Sligo, where his poetic sensibility was most productively at home. Much of the Dublin literary world regarded him with suspicion, if not outright hostility. Like many another Irish literary exile, Yeats, as R. F. Foster writes in his biography of the poet, was frequently portrayed 'as someone who had managed to fool opinion outside Ireland, but who would be seen for what he was "at home".'

In the final decade of the century his main critics and opponents were the members of the Young Ireland League, the surviving rump of the nationalist Young Ireland movement founded in the 1840s by Thomas Davis, John Blake Dillon and Charles Gavan Duffy. Yeats had wanted to extend the League to London and re-found it on strong Fenian principles, but the Irish Leaguers would have none of it. Gavan Duffy, a Catholic and a barrister, had emigrated to Australia in 1856 and in time had become Governor-General of Victoria; in 1881 he returned to Ireland, still a nationalist, but of a milder stamp than he had been in the rebellious 1840s. A collision was inevitable between the old-guardist Gavan Duffy and Yeats the Protestant champion of the new nationalism and patrician advocate of high art.

Under the aegis of the National Literary Society, Yeats sought to publish an influential and, not incidentally, lucrative library of classic Irish texts. Gavan Duffy outmanoeuvred him, however, and effectively took over the project. It was the end of what Foster describes as Yeats's plan 'to capture the National Literary Society and its Library for the Fenian interest, against the safe, all-embracing platitudes located in the middle of the nationalist road.' In the *Autobiographies*, Yeats took a personal revenge, writing of Gavan Duffy:

> One imaged his youth in some little gaunt Irish town, where no building or custom is revered for its antiquity, and there speaking a language where no word, even in solitude, is ever spoken slowly and carefully because of emotional implication; and of his manhood of practical politics, of the dirty piece of orange-peel in the corner of the stairs as one climbs up to some newspaper office; of public meetings where it would be treacherous amid so much geniality to speak or even to think of anything that might cause a moment's misunderstanding in one's own party. No argument of mine was intelligible to him . . .

Yeats saw his defeat by this old Young Irelander as, among other things, the triumph of old-style nationalist banality over true literary quality. He was fierce in his determination to banish the kind of bombastic versifying that had filled the pages of the Young Ireland newspaper, the *Nation*. The Celtic Twilight movement, of which he was the prime mover, was founded on the conviction that a new kind of poetry could be written in Ireland in the English tongue, which would be as authentically Irish as the work of the great Gaelic bards of antiquity. The readership that *A Book of Irish Verse* was aimed at was the 'leisured classes' who 'read little about any country, and nothing about Ireland.'

> We cannot move these classes from an apathy, come from their separation from the land they live in, by writing about politics or about Gaelic, but we may move them by becoming men of letters and expressing primary emotions and truths in ways appropriate to this country.

In his introduction to the book, Yeats mocked the 'insincere and

mechanical' verse of the Young Ireland leader, Thomas Davis—
'When he sat down to write he had so great a desire to make the
peasantry courageous and powerful that he half believed them
already "the finest peasantry upon the earth" '—and even took
critical swipes at James Clarence Mangan, a poet revered by
James Joyce, but who for Yeats was 'the slave of life, for he had
nothing of the self-knowledge, the power of selection, the harmony of mind, which enables the poet to be its master, and to
mould the world to a trumpet for his lips.'

Indeed, throughout his introduction Yeats is surprisingly
severe even on those poets whose verse he has chosen to include.
It seems almost that he has chosen them less for the quality of
their poetry than for the fact that they worked 'apart from politics.' Yet there are very many delights and treasures here, most of
which will be unfamiliar to readers of today. It would be foolish
to claim that these pages are replete with great poetry, but what
is exemplary is the determination of its compiler at least to
follow the road of excellence in making his choices. His aim was
to forge out of the English-language tradition in Irish poetry an
authentic literature, one fit for what he was convinced would be
a new, autonomous, modern Ireland, even if in his heart he was
fully alert to the ambiguities inherent in that verb, 'to forge'.

JOHN BANVILLE

Preface

I have not found it possible to revise this book as completely as I should have wished. I have corrected a bad mistake of a copyist, and added a few pages of new verses towards the end, and softened some phrases in the introduction which seemed a little petulant in form, and written in a few more to describe writers who have appeared during the last four years, and that is about all. I compiled it towards the end of a long indignant argument, carried on in the committee rooms of our literary societies, and in certain newspapers between a few writers of our new movement, who judged Irish literature by literary standards, and a number of people, a few of whom were writers, who judged it by its patriotism and by its political effect; and I hope my opinions may have value as part of an argument which may awaken again. The Young Ireland writers wrote to give the peasantry a literature in English in place of the literature they were losing with Gaelic, and these methods, which have shaped the literary thought of Ireland to our time, could not be the same as the methods of a movement which, so far as it is more than an instinctive expression of certain moods of the soul, endeavours to create a reading class among the more leisured classes, which will preoccupy itself with Ireland and the needs of Ireland. The peasants in eastern counties have their Young Ireland poetry, which is always good teaching and sometimes good poetry, and the peasants of the western counties have beautiful poems and stories in Gaelic, while our more leisured classes read little about any country, and nothing about Ireland. We cannot move these classes from an apathy, come from their separation from the land they live in, by writing about politics or about Gaelic, but we may move them by becoming men of letters and expressing primary emotions and truths in ways appropriate to this country. One carries on the traditions of Thomas Davis, towards whom our eyes must always turn, not less than the traditions of good literature, which are the morality of the man of letters, when one is content, like A. E., with fewer readers that one may follow a more hidden beauty; or when one endeavours, as I have endeavoured in this book, to separate what has literary value from what has only a patriotic and political value, no matter how sacred it has become to us.

The reader who would begin a serious study of modern Irish literature should do so with Mr Stopford Brooke's and Mr Rolleston's exhaustive anthology.

W. B. Y.
AUGUST 15, 1899

MODERN IRISH POETRY

The Irish Celt is sociable, as may be known from his proverb, 'Strife is better than loneliness,' and the Irish poets of the nineteenth century have made songs abundantly when friends and rebels have been at hand to applaud. The Irish poets of the eighteenth century found both at a Limerick hostelry, above whose door was written a rhyming welcome in Gaelic to all passing poets, whether their pockets were full or empty. Its owner, himself a famous poet, entertained his fellows as long as his money lasted, and then took to minding the hens and chickens of an old peasant woman for a living, and ended his days in rags, but not, one imagines, without content. Among his friends and guests had been O'Sullivan the Red, O'Sullivan the Gaelic, O'Heffernan the blind, and many another, and their songs had made the people, crushed by the disasters of the Boyne and Aughrim, remember their ancient greatness. The bardic order, with its perfect artifice and imperfect art, had gone down in the wars of the seventeenth century, and poetry had found shelter amid the turf-smoke of the cabins. The powers that history commemorates are but the coarse effects of influences delicate and vague as the beginning of twilight, and these influences were to be woven like a web about the hearts of men by farm-labourers, pedlars, potato-diggers, hedge-schoolmasters, and grinders at the quern, poor wastrels who put the troubles of their native land, or their own happy or unhappy loves, into songs of an extreme beauty. But in the midst of this beauty was a flitting incoherence, a fitful dying out of the sense, as though the passion had become too great for words, as must needs be when life is the master and not the slave of the singer.

English-speaking Ireland had meanwhile no poetic voice, for Goldsmith had chosen to celebrate English scenery and manners; and Swift was but an Irishman by what Mr Balfour has called the visitation of God, and much against his will; and Congreve by education and early association; while Parnell, Denham, and Roscommon were poets but to their own time. Nor did the coming with the new century of the fame of Moore set the balance even, for all but all of his Irish melodies are artificial and mechanical when separated from the music that gave them wings. Whatever he had of high poetry is in 'The Light of other Days,' and in 'At the Mid Hour of Night,' which express what Matthew Arnold has taught us to call 'the Celtic melancholy,' with so much of delicate beauty in the meaning and in the wavering or steady rhythm that one knows not where to find their like in literature. His more artificial and mechanical verse, because of the ancient music that makes it seem natural and vivid, and because it has remembered so many beloved names and events and places, has had the influence which might have belonged to these exquisite verses had he written none but these. An honest style did not come into English-speaking Ire-land, until Callanan wrote three or four naïve translations from the Gaelic. 'Shule Aroon' and 'Kathleen O'More' had indeed been written for a good while, but had no more influence than Moore's best verses. Now, however, the lead of Callanan was followed by a number of translators, and they in turn by the poets of 'Young Ireland,' who mingled a little learned from the Gaelic ballad-writers with a great deal learned from Scott, Macaulay, and Campbell, and turned poetry once again into a principal means for spreading ideas of nationality and patriotism. They were full of earnestness, but never understood that though a poet may govern his life by his enthusiasms, he must, when he sits down at his desk, but use them as the potter the clay. Their thoughts were a little insincere, because they lived in the half illusions of their admirable ideals; and their rhythms not seldom mechanical, because their purpose was served when they had satisfied the dull ears of the common man. They had no time to listen to the voice of the insatiable artist, who stands erect, or lies asleep waiting until a breath arouses him, in the heart of every craftsman. Life was their master, as it had been the master of the poets who gathered in the Limerick hostelry, though it conquered them not by unreasoned love for a woman, or for native land, but by reasoned enthusiasm, and practical energy. No man was more sincere, no man had a less mechanical mind than Thomas Davis, and yet he is often a little insincere and mechanical in his verse. When he sat down to write he had so great a desire to make the peasantry courageous and powerful that he half believed them already 'the finest peasantry upon the earth,' and wrote not a few such verses as

> 'Lead him to fight for native land,
>   His is no courage cold and wary;
> The troops live not that could withstand
>   The headlong charge of Tipperary,'

and to-day we are paying the reckoning with much bombast. His little book has many things of this kind, and yet we honour it for its public spirit, and recognise its powerful influence with gratitude. He was in the main an orator influencing men's acts, and not a poet shaping their emotions, and the bulk of his influence has been good. He was, indeed, a poet of much tenderness in the simple love-songs 'The Marriage,' 'A Plea for Love,' and 'Mary Bhan Astór,' and, but for his ideal of a Fisherman, defying a foreign soldiery, would have been as good in 'The Boatman of Kinsale'; and once or twice when he touched upon some historic sorrow he forgot his hopes for the future and his lessons for the present, and made moving verse. His contemporary, Clarence Mangan, kept out of public life and its half illusions by a passion for books, and for drink and opium, made an imaginative and powerful style. He translated from the German, and imitated Oriental poetry, but little that he did on any but Irish subjects is permanently interesting. He is usually classed with the Young Ireland poets, because he contributed to their periodicals and shared their political views; but his style was formed before their movement began, and he found it the more easy for this reason perhaps to give sincere expression to the mood which he had chosen, the only sincerity literature knows of; and with happiness and cultivation might have displaced Moore. But as it was, whenever he had no fine ancient song to inspire him, he fell into rhetoric which was only lifted out of commonplace by an arid intensity. In his 'Irish National Hymn,' 'Soul and Country,' and the like, we look into a mind full of parched sands where the sweet dews have never fallen. A miserable man may think well and express himself with great vehemence, but he cannot make beautiful things, for Aphrodite never rises from any but a tide of joy. Mangan knew nothing of the happiness of the outer man, and it was only when prolonging the tragic exultation of some dead bard, that he knew the unearthly happiness which clouds the outer man with sorrow, and is the fountain of impassioned art. Like those who had gone before him, he was the slave of life, for he had nothing of the self-knowledge, the power of selection, the harmony of mind, which enables the poet to be its master, and to mould the world to a trumpet for his lips. But

O'Hussey's Ode over his outcast chief must live for generations because of the passion that moves through its powerful images and its mournful, wayward, and fierce rhythms.

'Though he were even a wolf ranging the round green woods,
Though he were even a pleasant salmon in the unchainable sea,
Though he were a wild mountain eagle, he could soarce bear, he,
  This sharp, sore sleet, these howling floods.'

Edward Walsh, a village schoolmaster, who hovered, like Mangan, on the edge of the Young Ireland movement, did many beautiful translations from the Gaelic; and Michael Doheny, while out 'on his keeping' in the mountains after the collapse at Ballingarry, made one of the most moving of ballads; but in the main the poets who gathered about Thomas Davis, and whose work has come down to us in 'The Spirit of the Nation,' were of practical and political, not of literary importance.

Meanwhile Samuel Ferguson, William Allingham, and Mr Aubrey de Vere were working apart from politics, Ferguson selecting his subjects from the traditions of the Bardic age, and Allingham from those of his native Ballyshannon, and Mr Aubrey de Vere wavering between English, Irish, and Catholic tradition. They were wiser than Young Ireland in the choice of their models, for, while drawing not less from purely Irish sources, they turned to the great poets of the world, Mr de Vere owing something of his gravity to Wordsworth, Ferguson much of his simplicity to Homer, while Allingham had trained an ear, too delicate to catch the tune of but a single master, upon the lyric poetry of many lands. Allingham was the best artist, but Ferguson had the more ample imagination, the more epic aim. He had not the subtlety of feeling, the variety of cadence of a great lyric poet, but he has touched, here and there, an epic vastness and naïveté, as in the description in 'Congal' of the mire-stiffened mantle of the giant spectre Mananan macLir, striking against his calves with as loud a noise as the mainsail of a ship makes, 'when with the coil of all its ropes it beats the sounding mast.' He is frequently dull, for he often lacked the 'minutely appropriate words' necessary to embody those fine changes of feeling which enthral the attention; but his sense of weight and size, of action and tumult, has set him apart and solitary, an epic figure in a lyric age. Allingham, whose pleasant destiny has made him the poet of his native town, and put 'The Winding Banks of Erne' into the mouths of the ballad-singers of Ballyshannon, is, on the other hand, a master of 'minutely appropriate words,' and can wring from the luxurious sadness of the lover, from the austere sadness of old age, the last golden drop of beauty; but amid action and tumult he can but fold his hands. He is the poet of the melancholy peasantry of the West, and, as years go on, and voluminous histories and copious romances drop under the horizon, will take his place among those minor immortals who have put their souls into little songs to humble the proud. The poetry of Mr Aubrey de Vere has less architecture than the poetry of Ferguson and Allingham, and more meditation. Indeed, his few but ever memorable successes are enchanted islands in grey seas of stately impersonal reverie and description, which drift by and leave no definite recollection. One needs, perhaps, to perfectly enjoy him, a Dominican habit, a cloister, and a breviary.

These three poets published much of their best work before and during the Fenian movement, which, like 'Young Ireland,' had its poets, though but a small number. Charles Kickham, one of the 'triumvirate' that controlled it in Ireland; John Casey, a clerk in a flour-mill; and Ellen O'Leary, the sister of Mr John O'Leary, were at times very excellent. Their verse lacks, curiously enough, the oratorical vehemence of Young Ireland, and is plaintive and idyllic. The agrarian movement that followed produced but little poetry, and of that little all is forgotten but a vehement poem by Fanny Parnell, and a couple of songs by Mr T. D.

Sullivan, who is a good song-writer, though not, as the writer has read on an election placard, 'one of the greatest poets who ever moved the heart of man.' But while Nationalist verse has ceased to be a portion of the propaganda of a party, it has been written, and is being written, under the influence of the Nationalist newspapers and of Young Ireland societies and the like. With an exacting conscience, and better models than Thomas Moore and the Young Irelanders, such beautiful enthusiasm could not fail to make some beautiful verses. But, as things are, the rhythms are mechanical, and the metaphors conventional; and inspiration is too often worshipped as a Familiar who labours while you sleep, or forget, or do many worthy things which are not spiritual things. For the most part, the Irishman of our times loves so deeply those arts which build up a gallant personality, rapid writing, ready talking, effective speaking to crowds, that he has no thought for the arts which consume the personality in solitude. He loves the mortal arts which have given him a lure to take the hearts of men, and shrinks from the immortal, which could but divide him from his fellows. And in this century, he who does not strive to be a perfect craftsman achieves nothing. The poor peasant of the eighteenth century could make fine ballads by abandoning himself to the joy or sorrow of the moment, as the reeds abandon themselves to the wind which sighs through them, because he had about him a world where all was old enough to be steeped in emotion. But we cannot take to ourselves, by merely thrusting out our hands, all we need of pomp and symbol, and if we have not the desire of artistic perfection for an ark, the deluge of incoherence, vulgarity, and triviality will pass over our heads. If we had no other symbols but the tumult of the sea, the rusted gold of the thatch, the redness of the quicken-berry, and had never known the rhetoric of the platform and of the newspaper, we could do without laborious selection and rejection; but, even then, though we might do much that would be delightful, that would inspire coming times, it would not have the manner of the greatest poetry.

Here and there, the Nationalist newspapers and the Young Ireland societies have trained a writer who, though busy with the old models, has some imaginative energy; while Mr Lionel Johnson, Mrs Hinkson, Miss Nora Hopper, and A. E., the successors of Allingham and Ferguson and Mr de Vere, are more anxious to influence and understand Irish thought than any of their predecessors who did not take the substance of their poetry from politics. They are distinguished too by their deliberate art, and with their preoccupation with spiritual passions and memories. Mr Lionel Johnson and Mrs Hinkson are both Catholic and devout, but Mr Lionel Johnson's poetry is lofty and austere, and, like Mr de Vere's, never long forgets the greatness of his Church and the interior life whose expression it is, while Mrs Hinkson is happiest when she embodies emotions, that have the innocence of childhood, in symbols and metaphors from the green world about her. She has no reverie nor speculation, but a devout tenderness like that of S. Francis for weak instinctive things, old gardeners, old fishermen, birds among the leaves, birds tossed upon the waters. Miss Hopper belongs to that school of writers which embodies passions, that are not the less spiritual because no Church has put them into prayers, in stories and symbols from old Celtic poetry and mythology. The poetry of A. E., at its best, finds its symbols and its stories in the soul itself, and has a more disembodied ecstasy than any poetry of our time. He is the chief poet of the school of Irish mystics, which has shaped Mr Charles Weekes, who published recently, but withdrew immediately, a curious and subtle book, and Mr John Eglinton, who is best known for the orchestral harmonies of his 'Two Essays on the Remnant,' and certain younger writers who have heard the words, 'If ye know these things, happy are ye if ye do them,' and thought the labours that bring the mystic vision more important than the labours of any craft.

Except some few Catholic and mystical poets and Prof. Dowden in one or two poems, no Irishman living in Ireland has sung excellently of any but a theme from Irish experience, Irish history, or Irish tradition. Trinity College, which desires to be English, has been the mother of many verse-writers and of few poets; and this can only be because she has set herself against the national genius, and taught her children to imitate alien styles and choose out alien themes, for it is not possible to believe that the educated Irishman alone is prosaic and uninventive. Her few poets have been awakened by the influence of the farm-labourers, potato-diggers, pedlars, and hedge-schoolmasters of the eighteenth century, and their imitators in this, and not by a scholastic life, which, for reasons easy for all to understand and for many to forgive, has refused the ideals of Ireland, while those of England are but far-off murmurs. An enemy to all enthusiasms, because all enthusiasms seemed her enemies, she has taught her children to look neither to the world about them, nor into their own souls where some dangerous fire might slumber.

To remember that in Ireland the professional and landed classes have been through the mould of Trinity College or of English Universities, and are ignorant of the very names of the best writers in this book, is to know how strong a wind blows from the ancient legends of Ireland, how vigorous an impulse to create is in her heart to-day. Deserted by the classes from among whom have come the bulk of the world's intellect, she struggles on, gradually ridding herself of incoherence and triviality, and slowly building up a literature in English which, whether important or unimportant, grows always more unlike others; nor does it seem as if she would long lack a living literature in Gaelic, for the movement for the preservation of Gaelic, which has been so much more successful than anybody foresaw, has already its poets. Dr Hyde, who can only be represented here by some of his beautiful translations, has written Gaelic poems which pass from mouth to mouth in the west of Ireland. The country people have themselves fitted them to ancient airs, and many that can neither read nor write, sing them in Donegal and Connemara and Galway. I have, indeed, but little doubt that Ireland, communing with herself in Gaelic more and more, but speaking to foreign countries in English, will lead many that are sick with theories and with trivial emotion, to some sweet well-waters of primeval poetry.

W. B. Y.

The editor thanks Mr Aubrey de Vere, Mr T. W. Rolleston, Dr J. Todhunter, Mr Alfred Perceval Graves, Dr Douglas Hyde, Mr Lionel Johnson, A. E., Mr Charles Weekes, Mr John Eglinton, Mrs Hinkson, Miss Dora Sigerson (Mrs Clement Shortes), and Miss Nora Hopper for permission to quote from their poems, Lady Ferguson and Mrs Allingham for leave to give poems by Sir Samuel Ferguson and William Allingham, and Messrs Chatto & Windus for permission to include a song of Arthur O'Shaughnessy's. Two writers are excluded whom he would gladly have included—Casey, because the copyright holders have refused permission, and Mr George Armstrong, because his 'Songs of Wicklow,' when interesting, are too long for this book.

OLD AGE
From the 'Deserted Village'

In all my wanderings round this world of care,
In all my griefs—and God has given my share—
I still had hopes my later hours to crown,
Amidst these humble bowers to lay me down;
To husband out life's taper at the close
And keep the flame from wasting by repose;
I still had hopes, for pride attends us still,
Amidst the swains to show my book-learned skill
Around my fire an evening group to draw,
And tell of all I felt, and all I saw;
And, as a hare whom hounds and horns pursue,
Pants to the place from whence at first he flew,
I still had hopes, my long vexations past,
Here to return—and die at home at last.

Oliver Goldsmith

THE VILLAGE PREACHER
From the 'Deserted Village'

Near yonder copse, where once the garden smil'd,
And still where many a garden flower grows wild;
There, where a few torn shrubs the place disclose,
The village Preacher's modest mansion rose.
A man he was to all the country dear,
And passing rich with forty pounds a year;
Remote from towns he ran his godly race,
Nor e'er had changed, nor wish'd to change, his place
Unpractis'd he to fawn, or seek for power,
By doctrines fashion'd to the varying hour;

Far other aims his heart had learn'd to prize,
More skill'd to raise the wretched than to rise.
His house was known to all the vagrant train,
He chid their wanderings, but reliev'd their pain;
The long-remember'd beggar was his guest,
Whose beard descending swept his aged breast;
The ruined spendthrift, now no longer proud,
Claimed kindred there, and had his claims allow'd;
The broken soldier, kindly bade to stay,
Sat by his fire, and talked the night away;
Wept o'er his wounds, or tales of sorrow done,
Shouldered his crutch, and showed how fields were won
Pleased with his guests, the good man learned to glow
And quite forgot their vices in their woe;
Careless their merits or their faults to scan,
He pity gave ere charity began.

Oliver Goldsmith

THE DESERTER'S MEDITATION

If sadly thinking, with spirits sinking,
    Could, more than drinking, my cares compose,
A cure for sorrow from sighs I'd borrow,
    And hope to-morrow would end my woes.

But as in wailing there's nought availing,
    And Death unfailing will strike the blow,
Then for that reason, and for a season,
    Let us be merry before we go!

To joy a stranger, a wayworn ranger,
    In every danger my course I've run;
Now hope all ending, and death befriending,
    His last aid lending, my cares are done;

No more a rover, or hapless lover—
  My griefs are over—my glass runs low;
Then for that reason, and for a season,
  Let us be merry before we go!

John Philpot Curran

THOU CANST NOT BOAST

Thou canst not boast of Fortune's store,
  My love, while me they wealthy call:
But I was glad to find thee poor,
  For with my heart I'd give thee all,
    And then the grateful youth shall own,
    I loved him for himself alone.

But when his worth my hand shall gain,
  No word or look of mine shall show
That I the smallest thought retain
  Of what my bounty did bestow:
    Yet still his grateful heart shall own,
    I loved him for himself alone.

Richard Brinsley Sheridan

KATHLEEN O'MORE

My love, still I think that I see her once more,
But, alas! she has left me her loss to deplore—
  My own little Kathleen, my poor little Kathleen,
    My Kathleen O'More!

Her hair glossy black, her eyes were dark blue,
Her colour still changing, her smiles ever new—
  So pretty was Kathleen, my sweet little Kathleen,
    My Kathleen O'More!

She milked the dun cow, that ne'er offered to stir;
Though wicked to all, it was gentle to her—
　　So kind was my Kathleen, my poor little Kathleen,
　　　　My Kathleen O'More!

She sat at the door one cold afternoon,
To hear the wind blow, and to gaze on the moon,
　　So pensive was Kathleen, my poor little Kathleen,
　　　　My Kathleen O'More!

Cold was the night-breeze that sighed round her bower,
It chilled my poor Kathleen, she drooped from that hour:
　　And I lost my poor Kathleen, my own little Kathleen,
　　　　My Kathleen O'More.

The Bird of all birds that I love the best,
Is the Robin that in the churchyard builds his nest;
　　For he seems to watch Kathleen, hops lightly o'er Kathleen,
　　　　My Kathleen O'More.

James Nugent Reynolds

THE GROVES OF BLARNEY

The groves of Blarney
They look so charming
Down by the purling
　Of sweet, silent brooks,
Being banked with posies
That spontaneous grow there,
Planted in order
　By the sweet rock close.

'Tis there's the daisy
And the sweet carnation,

The blooming pink,
　　And the rose so fair,
The daffydowndilly,
Likewise the lily,
All flowers that scent
　　The sweet, fragrant air.

'Tis Lady Jeffers
That owns this station;
Like Alexander,
　　Or Queen Helen fair.
There's no commander
In all the nation,
For emulation,
　　Can with her compare.
Such walls surround her
That no nine-pounder
Could dare to plunder
　　Her place of strength;
But Oliver Cromwell
Her he did pommell,
And made a breach
　　In her battlement.

There's gravel walks there
For speculation
And conversation
　　In sweet solitude.
'Tis there the lover
May hear the dove, or
The gentle plover
　　In the afternoon;
And if a lady
Would be so engaging

As to walk alone in
   Those shady bowers,
'Tis there the courtier
He may transport her
Into some fort, or
   All under ground.

For 'tis there's a cave where
No daylight enters,
But cats and badgers
   Are for ever bred;
Being mossed by nature,
That makes it sweeter
Than a coach-and-six or
   A feather bed.
'Tis there the lake is,
Well stored with perches,
And comely eels in
   The verdant mud;
Beside the leeches,
And groves of beeches,
Standing in order
   For to guard the flood.

There's statues gracing
This noble place in—
All heathen gods
   And nymphs so fair;
Bold Neptune, Plutarch,
And Nicodemus,
All standing naked
   In the open air.
So now to finish
This brave narration,

Which my poor genii
Could not entwine;
But were I Homer
Or Nebuchadnezzar,
'Tis in every feature
I would make it shine.

Richard Alfred Milliken

THE LIGHT OF OTHER DAYS

Oft in the stilly night,
Ere slumber's chain has bound me,
Fond Memory brings the light
Of other days around me:
The smiles, the tears
Of boyhood's years,
The words of love then spoken;
The eyes that shone
Now dimm'd and gone,
The cheerful homes now broken!
Then in the stilly night,
Ere slumber's chain hath bound me,
Sad Memory brings the light
Of other days around me.

When I remember all
The friends so linked together
I've seen around me fall
Like leaves in wintry weather,
I feel like one
Who treads alone
Some banquet-hall deserted,
Whose lights are fled,

Whose garlands dead,
And all but he departed.
Then in the stilly night,
Ere slumber's chain hath bound me,
Sad Memory brings the light
Of other days around me.

Thomas Moore

AT THE MID HOUR OF NIGHT

At the mid hour of night, when stars are weeping, I fly
To the lone vale we loved, when life shone warm in thine eye;
And I think oft, if spirits can steal from the regions of air
To revisit past scenes of delight, thou wilt come to me there,
And tell me our love is remembered even in the sky!

Then I sing the wild song it once was rapture to hear
When our voices, commingling, breathed like one on the ear;
And as Echo far off through the vale my sad orison rolls,
I think, O my love! 'tis thy voice from the kingdom of souls
Faintly answering still the notes that once were so dear.

Thomas Moore

THE BURIAL OF SIR JOHN MOORE

Not a drum was heard, not a funeral-note,
As his corse to the rampart we hurried;
Not a soldier discharged his farewell shot
O'er the grave where our hero we buried.

We buried him darkly at dead of night,
The sods with our bayonets turning,
By the struggling moonbeam's misty light,
And the lantern dimly burning.

No useless coffin enclosed his breast,
    Not in sheet or in shroud we wound him;
But he lay like a warrior taking his rest,
    With his martial cloak around him.

Few and short were the prayers we said,
    And we spoke not a word of sorrow;
But we steadfastly gazed on the face that was dead,
    And we bitterly thought of the morrow.

We thought as we hollow'd his narrow bed,
    And smooth'd down his lonely pillow,
That the foe and the stranger would tread o'er his head,
    And we far away on the billow!

Lightly they'll talk of the spirit that's gone,
    And o'er his cold ashes upbraid him,—
But little he'll reck, if they let him sleep on
    In the grave where a Briton has laid him.

But half of our heavy task was done,
    When the clock struck the hour for retiring;
And we heard the distant and random gun
    That the foe was sullenly firing.

Slowly and sadly we laid him down,
    From the field of his fame fresh and gory;
We carved not a line, and we raised not a stone—
    But we left him alone in his glory.

                                        Rev. Charles Wolfe

THE CONVICT OF CLONMELL
From the Irish

How hard is my fortune,
    And vain my repining!

The strong rope of fate
  For this young neck is twining.
My strength is departed;
  My cheek sunk and sallow;
While I languish in chains,
  In the gaol of *Cluanmeala*.

No boy in the village
  Was ever yet milder,
I'd play with a child,
  And my sport would be wilder.
I'd dance without tiring
  From morning till even,
And the goal-ball I'd strike
  To the lightning of Heaven.

At my bed-foot decaying,
  My hurlbat is lying,
Through the boys of the village
  My goal-ball is flying;
My horse 'mong the neighbours
  Neglected may fallow,—
While I pine in my chains,
  In the goal of *Cluanmeala*.

Next Sunday the patron
  At home will be keeping,
And the young active hurlers
  The field will be sweeping.
With the dance of fair maidens
  The evening they'll hallow,
While this heart, once so gay,
  Shall be cold in *Cluanmeala*.

                    Jeremiah Joseph Callanan

THE OUTLAW OF LOCH LENE
From the Irish

O, many a day have I made good ale in the glen,
That came not of stream or malt;—like the brewing of men.
My bed was the ground; my roof, the greenwood above,
And the wealth that I sought one far kind glance from my love.

Alas! on that night when the horses I drove from the field,
That I was not near from terror my angel to shield.
She stretched forth her arms,—her mantle she flung to the
    wind,
And swam o'er Loch Lene, her outlawed lover to find.

O would that a freezing sleet-wing'd tempest did sweep,
And I and my love were alone, far off on the deep;
I'd ask not a ship, or a bark, or pinnace, to save,—
With her hand round my waist, I'd fear not the wind or the
    wave.

'Tis down by the lake where the wild tree fringes its sides,
The maid of my heart, my fair one of Heaven resides;—
I think as at eve she wanders its mazes along,
The birds go to sleep by the sweet wild twist of her song.

Jeremiah Joseph Callanan

DIRGE OF O'SULLIVAN BEAR
From the Irish

The sun on Ivera
    No longer shines brightly,
The voice of her music
    No longer is sprightly;

No more to her maidens
   The light dance is dear,
Since the death of our darling
   O'Sullivan Bear.

Scully! thou false one,
   You basely betrayed him,
In his strong hour of need,
   When thy right hand should aid him;
He fed thee—he clad thee—
   You had all could delight thee:
You left him—you sold him—
   May Heaven requite thee!

Scully! may all kinds
   Of evil attend thee!
On thy dark road of life
   May no kind one befriend thee!
May fevers long burn thee,
   And agues long freeze thee!
May the strong hand of God
   In His red anger seize thee!

Had he died calmly,
   I would not deplore him;
Or if the wild strife
   Of the sea-war closed o'er him:
But with ropes round his white limbs
   Through ocean to trail him,
Like a fish after slaughter—
   'Tis therefore I wail him.

Long may the curse
   Of his people pursue them;
Scully, that sold him,
   And soldier that slew him!

One glimpse of heaven's light
   May they see never!
May the hearthstone of hell
   Be their best bed for ever!

In the hole which the vile hands
   Of soldiers had made thee,
Unhonour'd, unshrouded,
   And headless they laid thee;
No sigh to regret thee,
   No eye to rain o'er thee,
No dirge to lament thee,
   No friend to deplore thee!

Dear head of my darling,
   How gory and pale,
These aged eyes see thee,
   High spiked on their gaol!
That cheek in the summer sun
   Ne'er shall grow warm;
Nor that eye e'er catch light,
   But the flash of the storm.

A curse, blessed ocean,
   Is on thy green water,
From the haven of Cork
   To Ivera of slaughter:
Since thy billows were dyed
   With the red wounds of fear
Of Muiertach Oge,
   Our O'Sullivan Bear!

Jeremiah Joseph Callanan

LOVE SONG

Sweet in her green dell the flower of beauty slumbers,
  Lulled by the faint breezes sighing through her hair;
Sleeps she and hears not the melancholy numbers
  Breathed to my sad lute 'mid the lonely air.

Down from the high cliffs the rivulet is teeming
  To wind round the willow banks that lure him from above;
O that in tears, from my rocky prison streaming,
  I too could glide to the bower of my love!

Ah, where the woodbines with sleepy arms have wound her,
  Opes she her eyelids at the dream of my lay,
Listening, like the dove, while the fountains echo round her,
  To her lost mate's call in the forests far away.

Come then, my bird! For the peace thou ever bearest,
  Still heaven's messenger of comfort to me,
Come, this fond bosom, O faithfulest and fairest
  Bleeds with its death-wound its wound of love for thee!

George Darley

THE WHISTLIN' THIEF

When Pat came over the hill,
  His colleen fair to see,
His whistle low, but shrill,
  The signal was to be;
        (*Pat whistles.*)

'Mary,' the mother said,
  'Some one is whistling sure;'
Says Mary, ''Tis only the wind
  Is whistling through the door.'
      (*Pat whistles a bit of a popular air.*)

'I've lived a long time, Mary,
　　In this wide world, my dear,
But a door to whistle like *that*
　　I never yet did hear.'

'But, mother, you know the fiddle
　　Hangs close beside the chink,
And the wind upon the strings
　　Is playing the tune I think.'
　　　　　　　　　　(*The pig grunts.*)

'Mary, I hear the pig,
　　Unaisy in his mind.'
'But, mother, you know, they say
　　The pigs can see the wind.'

'That's true enough *in the day*,
　　But I think you may remark,
That pigs no more nor we
　　Can see anything in the dark.'
　　　　　　　　　　(*The dog barks.*)

'The dog is barking now,
　　The fiddle can't play the tune.'
'But, mother, the dogs will bark
　　Whenever they see the moon.'

'But how could he see the moon,
　　When, you know, the dog is blind?
Blind dogs won't bark at the moon,
　　Nor fiddles be played by the wind.

'I'm not such a fool as you think,
　　I know very well it is Pat:—
Shut your mouth, you whistlin' thief,
　　And go along home out o' that!

'And you be off to your bed,
  Don't play upon me your jeers;
For though I have lost my eyes,
  I haven't lost my ears!'

Samuel Lover

SOGGARTH AROON

Am I the slave they say,
    Soggarth aroon?
Since you did show the way,
    Soggarth aroon,
Their slave no more to be,
While they would work with me
Old Ireland's slavery,
    Soggarth aroon.

Why not her poorest man,
    Soggarth aroon,
Try and do all he can,
    Soggarth aroon,
Her commands to fulfil
Of his own heart and will,
Side by side with you still
    Soggarth aroon?

Loyal and brave to you,
    Soggarth aroon,
Yet be not slave to you,
    Soggarth aroon,
Nor, out of fear to you—
Stand up so near to you—
Och! out of fear to you,
    Soggarth aroon!

Who, in the winter's night,
    Soggarth aroon,
When the cold blast did bite,
    Soggarth aroon,
Came to my cabin-door,
And, on my earthen-floor,
Knelt by me, sick and poor,
    Soggarth aroon?

Who, on the marriage day,
    Soggarth aroon,
Made the poor cabin gay,
    Soggarth aroon?—
And did both laugh and sing,
Making our hearts to ring,
At the poor christening,
    Soggarth aroon?

Who, as friend only met,
    Soggarth aroon,
Never did flout me yet,
    Soggarth aroon?
And when my heart was dim,
Gave, while his eye did brim,
What I should give to him,
    Soggarth aroon?

Och! you, and only you,
    Soggarth aroon!
And for this I was true to you,
    Soggarth aroon,
In love they'll never shake,
When for old Ireland's sake,
We a true part did take,
    Soggarth aroon!

John Banim

DARK ROSALEEN
From the Irish

O my Dark Rosaleen,
    Do not sigh, do not weep!
The priests are on the ocean green.
    They march along the deep.
There's wine from the royal Pope,
    Upon the ocean green;
And Spanish ale shall give you hope,
    My Dark Rosaleen!
    My own Rosaleen!
Shall glad your heart, shall give you hope,
Shall give you health, and help, and hope,
    My Dark Rosaleen!

Over hills, and through dales,
    Have I roamed for your sake;
All yesterday I sailed with sails
    On river and on lake,
The Erne, at its highest flood,
    I dashed across unseen,
For there was lightning in my blood,
    My Dark Rosaleen!
    My own Rosaleen!
O there was lightning in my blood,
Red lightning lightened through my blood,
    My Dark Rosaleen!

All day long in unrest
    To and fro do I move,
The very heart within my breast
    Is wasted for you, Love!
The heart in my bosom faints
    To think of you, my queen!

My life of life, my saint of saints,
   My Dark Rosaleen!
   My own Rosaleen!
To hear your sweet and sad complaints,
My life, my love, my saint of saints,
   My Dark Rosaleen!

Woe and pain, pain and woe,
   Are my lot night and noon;
To see your bright face clouded so,
   Like to the mournful moon.
But yet will I rear your throne
   Again in golden sheen:
'Tis you shall reign, shall reign alone,
   My Dark Rosaleen!
   My own Rosaleen!
'Tis you shall have the golden throne,
'Tis you shall reign, and reign alone,
   My Dark Rosaleen!

Over dews, over sands,
   Will I fly for your weal:
Your holy, delicate white hands
   Shall girdle me with steel.
At home, in your emerald bowers,
   From morning's dawn till e'en,
You'll pray for me, my flower of flowers,
   My Dark Rosaleen!
   My fond Rosaleen!
You'll think of me through daylight's hours,
My virgin flower, my flower of flowers,
   My Dark Rosaleen!

I could scale the blue air,
   I could plough the high hills,

O, I could kneel all night in prayer,
  To heal your many ills.
And one beamy smile from you
  Would float like light between
My toils and me, my own, my true,
  My Dark Rosaleen!
  My fond Rosaleen!
Would give me life and soul anew,
A second life, a soul anew,
  My Dark Rosaleen!

O! the Erne shall run red
  With redundance of blood,
The earth shall rock beneath our tread,
  And flames wrap hill and wood,
And gun-peal, and slogan cry,
  Wake many a glen serene,
Ere you shall fade, ere you shall die,
  My Dark Rosaleen!
  My own Rosaleen!
The Judgment Hour must first be nigh
Ere you can fade, ere you can die,
  My Dark Rosaleen!

James Clarence Mangan

LAMENT FOR THE PRINCES OF TYRONE
AND TYRCONNELL
From the Irish

O woman of the Piercing Wail,
  Who mournest o'er yon mound of clay
    With sigh and groan,

Would God thou wert among the Gael!
   Thou wouldst not then from day to day
      Weep thus alone.
'Twere long before, around a grave
   In green Tyrconnell, one could find
      This loneliness;
Near where Beann-Boirche's banners wave
   Such grief as thine could ne'er have pined
      Companionless.

Beside the wave in Donegal,
   In Antrim's glens, or fair Dromore,
      Or Killillee.
Or where the sunny waters fall
At Assaroe, near Erna's shore,
      This could not be.
On Derry's plains—in rich Drumclieff—
   Throughout Armagh the Great, renowned
      In olden years,
No day could pass but woman's grief
   Would rain upon the burial-ground
      Fresh floods of tears!

O, no!—from Shannon, Boyne, and Suir,
   From high Dunluce's castle-walls,
      From Lissadill,
Would flock alike both rich and poor,
   One wail would rise from Cruachan's halls
      To Tara's hill;
And some would come from Barrow-side,
   And many a maid would leave her home,
      On Leitrim's plains,
And by melodious Banna's tide,
   And by the Mourne and Erne, to come
      And swell thy strains!

O, horses' hoofs would trample down
　　The Mount whereon the martyr-saint
　　　　Was crucified.
From glen and hill, from plain and town,
　　One loud lament, one thrilling plaint,
　　　　Would echo wide.
There would not soon be found, I ween,
　　One foot of ground among those bands
　　　　For museful thought,
So many shriekers of the keen
　　Would cry aloud and clap their hands,
　　　　All woe distraught!

Two princes of the line of Conn
　　Sleep in their cells of clay beside
　　　　O'Donnell Roe;
Three royal youths, alas! are gone,
　　Who lived for Erin's weal, but died
　　　　For Erin's woe;
Ah! could the men of Ireland read
　　The names these noteless burial-stones
　　　　Display to view,
Their wounded hearts afresh would bleed,
　　Their tears gush forth again, their groans
　　　　Resound anew!

The youths whose relics moulder here
　　Were sprung from Hugh, high Prince and Lord
　　　　Of Aileach's lands;
Thy noble brothers, justly dear,
　　Thy nephew, long to be deplored
　　　　By Ulster's bands.
Theirs were not souls wherein dull Time
　　Could domicile Decay or house
　　　　Decrepitude!

They passed from Earth ere Manhood's prime,
    Ere years had power to dim their brows
            Or chill their blood.

And who can marvel o'er thy grief,
    Or who can blame thy flowing tears,
            That knows their source?
O'Donnell, Dunnasava's chief,
    Cut off amid his vernal years,
            Lies here a corse
Beside his brother Cathbar, whom
    Tirconnell of the Helmets mourns
            In deep despair—
For valour, truth, and comely bloom,
    For all that greatens and adorns
            A peerless pair.

O, had these twain, and he, the third,
    The Lord of Mourne, O'Niall's son,
            Their mate in death—
A prince in look, in deed and word—
    Had these three heroes yielded on
            The field their breath,
O, had they fallen on Criffan's plain,
    There would not be a town or clan
            From shore to sea,
But would with shrieks bewail the slain,
    Or chant aloud the exulting rann
            Of Jubilee!

When high the shout of battle rose,
    On fields where Freedom's torch still burned
            Through Erin's gloom,
If one, if barely one of those
    Were slain, all Ulster would have mourned
            The hero's doom!

If at Athboy, where hosts of brave
   Ulidian horsemen sank beneath
      The shock of spears,
Young Hugh O'Neill had found a grave,
   Long must the North have wept his death
      With heart-wrung tears!

If on the day of Ballach-myre
   The Lord of Mourne had met thus young,
      A warrior's fate,
In vain would such as thou desire
   To mourn, alone, the champion sprung
      From Niall the Great!
No marvel this—for all the dead,
   Heaped on the field, pile over pile,
      At Mullach-brack,
Were scarce an eric for his head,
   If death had stayed his footsteps while
      On victory's track!

If on the Day of Hostages
   The fruit had from the parent bough
      Been rudely torn
In sight of Munster's bands—Mac-Nee's—
   Such blow the blood of Conn, I trow,
      Could ill have borne.
If on the day of Ballach-boy
   Some arm had laid, by foul surprise,
      The chieftain low,
Even our victorious shout of joy
   Would soon give place to rueful cries
      And groans of woe!

If on the day the Saxon host
   Were forced to fly—a day so great
      For Ashanee—

The Chief had been untimely lost,
  Our conquering troops should moderate
      Their mirthful glee.
There would not lack on Lifford's day,
  From Galway, from the glens of Boyle,
      From Limerick's towers,
A marshalled file, a long array
  Of mourners to bedew the soil
      With tears in showers!

If on the day a sterner fate
  Compelled his flight from Athenree,
      His blood had flowed,
What numbers all disconsolate,
  Would come unasked, and share with thee
      Affliction's load!
If Derry's crimson field had seen
  His life-blood offered up, though 'twere
      On Victory's shrine,
A thousand cries would swell the keen,
  A thousand voices of despair
      Would echo thine.

O, had the fierce Dalcassian swarm
  That bloody night on Fergus' banks
      But slain our chief,
When rose his camp in wild alarm—
  How would the triumph of his ranks
      Be dashed with grief!
How would the troops of Murbach mourn
  If on the Curlew Mountains' day,
      Which England rued,
Some Saxon hand had left them lorn,
  By shedding there, amid the fray,
      Their prince's blood!

Red would have been our warriors' eyes
  Had Roderick found on Sligo field
    A gory grave,
No Northern Chief would soon arise,
  So sage to guide, so strong to shield,
    So swift to save.
Long would Leith-Cuinn have wept if Hugh
  Had met the death he oft had dealt
    Among the foe;
But, had our Roderick fallen too,
  All Erin must, alas! have felt
    The deadly blow!

What do I say? Ah, woe is me!
  Already we bewail in vain
    Their fatal fall!
And Erin, once the Great and Free,
  Now vainly mourns her breakless chain,
    And iron thrall!
Then, daughter of O'Donnell! dry
  Thine overflowing eyes, and turn
    Thy heart aside;
For Adam's race is born to die,
  And sternly the sepulchral urn
    Mocks human pride!

Look not, nor sigh, for earthly throne,
  Nor place thy trust in arm of clay—
    But on thy knees
Uplift thy soul to God alone,
  For all things go their destined way
    As He decrees.
Embrace the faithful Crucifix,
  And seek the path of pain and prayer
    Thy Saviour trod!

Nor let thy spirit intermix
  With earthly hope and worldly care
    Its groans to God!

And Thou, O mighty Lord! whose ways
  Are far above our feeble minds
    To understand,
Sustain us in these doleful days,
  And render light the chain that binds
    Our fallen land!
Look down upon our dreary state,
  And through the ages that may still
    Roll sadly on,
Watch Thou o'er hapless Erin's fate,
  And shield at least from darker ill
    The blood of Conn!

James Clarence Mangan

A LAMENTATION FOR THE DEATH OF SIR MAURICE FITZGERALD, KNIGHT OF KERRY
From the Irish

There was lifted up one voice of woe,
  One lament of more than mortal grief,
Through the wide South to and fro,
  For a fallen Chief.
In the dead of night that cry thrilled through me,
  I looked out upon the midnight air;
Mine own soul was all as gloomy,
  And I knelt in prayer.

O'er Loch Gur, that night, once—twice—yea, thrice—
  Passed a wail of anguish for the Brave,

That half curled into ice
   The moon-mirroring wave.
Then uprose a many-toned wild hymn in
   Choral swell from Ogra's dark ravine,
And Moguly's Phantom Women
   Mourned the Geraldine!

Far on Carah Mona's emerald plains,
   Shrieks and sighs were blended many hours,
And Fermoy, in fitful strains,
   Answered from her towers.
Youghal, Keenalmeaky, Eemokilly,
   Mourned in concert, and their piercing *keen*
Woke to wondering life the stilly
   Glens of Inchiqueen.

From Loughmoe to yellow Dunanore
   There was fear; the traders of Tralee
Gathered up their golden store,
   And prepared to flee;
For, in ship and hall, from night till morning
   Showed the first faint beamings of the sun,
All the foreigners heard the warning
   Of the Dreaded One!

'This,' they spake, 'portendeth death to us,
   If we fly not swiftly from our fate!'
Self-conceited idiots! thus
   Ravingly to prate!
Not for base-born higgling Saxon trucksters
   Ring laments like those by shore and sea!
Not for churls with souls of hucksters
   Waileth our Banshee!

For the high Milesian race alone
   Ever flows the music of her woe!

For slain heir to bygone throne,
    And for Chief laid low!
Hark! . . . Again, methinks, I hear her weeping
    Yonder! Is she near me now, as then?
Or was but the night-wind sweeping
    Down the hollow glen?

James Clarence Mangan

THE WOMAN OF THREE COWS
From the Irish

O, Woman of Three Cows, *agragh*! don't let your tongue thus
    rattle!
O, don't be saucy, don't be stiff, because you may have cattle.
I have seen—and, here's my hand to you, I only say what's
    true—
A many a one with twice your stock not half so proud as you.

Good luck to you, don't scorn the poor, and don't be their
    despiser;
For worldly wealth soon melts away, and cheats the very miser;
And death soon strips the proudest wreath from haughty human
    brows,
Then don't be stiff, and don't be proud, good Woman of Three
    Cows!

See where Momonia's heroes lie, proud Owen More's
    descendants,
'Tis they that won the glorious name, and had the grand
    attendants!
If *they* were forced to bow to Fate, as every mortal bows,
Can *you* be proud, can *you* be stiff, my Woman of Three Cows?

The brave sons of the Lord of Clare, they left the land to
  mourning;
Mavrone! for they were banished, with no hope of their
  returning—
Who knows in what abodes of want those youths were driven to
  house?
Yet *you* can give yourself these airs, O Woman of Three Cows!

O, think of Donnel of the Ships, the Chief whom nothing
  daunted—
See how he fell in distant Spain, unchronicled, unchanted!
He sleeps, the great O'Sullivan, where thunder cannot rouse—
Then ask yourself, should *you* be proud, good Woman of Three
  Cows?

O'Ruark, Maguire, those souls of fire, whose names are shrined
  in story—
Think how their high achievements once made Erin's greatest
  glory—
Yet now their bones lie mouldering under weeds and cyprus
  boughs,
And so, for all your pride, will yours, O Woman of Three Cows!

Th' O'Carrols, also, famed when fame was only for the boldest,
Rest in forgotten sepulchres with Erin's best and oldest;
Yet who so great as they of yore in battle or carouse?
Just think of that, and hide your head, good Woman of Three
  Cows!

Your neighbour's poor, and you, it seems, are big with vain
  ideas,
Because, *inagh!* you've got three cows, one more, I see, than *she*
  has;
That tongue of yours wags more at times than charity allows—
But, if you're strong, be merciful, great Woman of Three Cows!

The summing-up

Now, there you go! You still, of course, keep up your scornful
   bearing,
And I'm too poor to hinder you; but, by the cloak I'm wearing,
If I had but four cows myself, even though you were my spouse,
I'd thwack you well to cure your pride, my Woman of Three
   Cows!

James Clarence Mangan

PRINCE ALFRID'S ITINERARY THROUGH IRELAND
From the Irish

I found in Innisfail the fair,
In Ireland, while in exile there,
Women of worth, both grave and gay men,
Many clerics and many laymen.

I travelled its fruitful provinces round
And in every one of the five I found,
Alike in church and in palace hall,
Abundant apparel, and food for all.

Gold and silver I found, and money,
Plenty of wheat and plenty of honey;
I found God's people rich in pity,
Found many a feast and many a city.

I also found in Armagh, the splendid,
Meekness, wisdom, and prudence blended,
Fasting, as Christ hath recommended,
And noble councillors untranscended.

I found in each great church moreo'er,
Whether on island or on shore
Piety, learning, fond affection,
Holy welcome and kind protection.

I found thy good lay monks and brothers
Ever beseeching help for others,
And in their keeping the holy word
Pure as it came from Jesus the Lord.

I found in Munster unfettered of any,
Kings and queens and poets a many—
Poets were skilled in music and measure,
Prosperous doings, mirth and pleasure.

I found in Connaught the just, redundance
Of riches, milk in lavish abundance,
Hospitality, vigour, fame,
In Cruachan's land of heroic name.

I found in the county of Connall the glorious
Bravest heroes, ever victorious;
Fair-complexioned men and warlike,
Ireland's lights, the high, the starlike.

I found in Ulster, from hill to glen,
Hardy warriors, resolute men;
Beauty that bloomed when youth was gone,
And strength transmitted from sire to son.

I found in the noble district of Boyle

(*MS. here illegible.*)

Brehons, erenachs, weapons bright,
And horsemen bold and sudden in fight.

I found in Leinster the smooth and sleek,
From Dublin to Slewmargy's peak;
Flourishing pastures, valour, health,
Long-living worthies, commerce, wealth.

I found, besides, from Ara to Glea,
In the broad rich country of Ossorie,

Sweet fruits, good laws for all and each,
Great chess players, men of truthful speech.

I found in Meath's fair principality,
Virtue, vigour, and hospitality;
Candour, joyfulness, bravery, purity,
Ireland's bulwark and security.

I found strict morals in age and youth,
I found historians recording truth;
The things I sing of in verse unsmooth,
I found them all—I have written sooth.

James Clarence Mangan

O'HUSSEY'S ODE TO THE MAGUIRE
From the Irish

Where is my Chief, my Master, this bleak night, *mavrone*!
O, cold, cold, miserably cold is this bleak night for Hugh,
Its showery, arrowy, speary sleet pierceth one through and
through,
Pierceth one to the very bone!

Rolls real thunder? Or was that red, livid light
Only a meteor? I scarce know; but through the midnight dim
The pitiless ice-wind streams. Except the hate that persecutes him
Nothing hath crueler venomy might.

An awful, a tremendous night is this, meseems!
The flood-gates of the river of heaven, I think, have been burst
wide—
Down from the overcharged clouds, like unto headlong ocean's
tide,
Descends grey rain in roaring streams.

Though he were even a wolf ranging the round green woods,
Though he were even a pleasant salmon in the unchainable sea,
Though he were a wild mountain eagle, he could scarce bear, he,
This sharp, sore sleet, these howling floods.

O mournful is my soul this night for Hugh Maguire!
Darkly, as in a dream he strays! Before him and behind
Triumphs the tyrannous anger of the wounding wind,
The wounding wind, that burns as fire!

It is my bitter grief—it cuts me to the heart—
That in the country of Clan Darry this should be his fate!
O, woe is me, where is he? Wandering, houseless, desolate,
Alone, without or guide or chart!

Medreams I see just now his face, the strawberry-bright,
Uplifted to the blackened heavens, while the tempestuous winds
Blow fiercely over and round him, and the smiting sleet-shower
    blinds
The hero of Galang to-night!

Large, large affliction unto me and mine it is,
That one of his majestic bearing, his fair, stately form,
Should thus be tortured and o'erborne—that this unsparing
    storm
Should wreak its wrath on head like his!

That his great hand, so oft the avenger of the oppressed,
Should this chill churlish night, perchance, be paralyzed by
    frost—
While through some icicle-hung thicket—as one lorn and lost—
He walks and wanders without rest.

The tempest-driven torrent deluges the mead,
It overflows the low banks of the rivulets and ponds—
The lawns and pasture-grounds lie looked in icy bonds
So that the cattle cannot feed.

The pale bright margins of the streams are seen by none,
Rushes and sweeps along the untamable flood on every side—
It penetrates and fills the cottagers' dwellings far and wide—
Water and land are blent in one.

Through some dark wood, 'mid bones of monsters, Hugh now
strays,
As he confronts the storm with anguished heart, but manly
brow—
O, what a sword-wound to that tender heart of his were now
A backward glance of peaceful days.

But other thoughts are his—thoughts that can still inspire
With joy and onward-bounding hope the bosom of Mac-Nee—
Thoughts of his warriors charging like bright billows of the sea,
Borne on the wind's wings, flashing fire!

And though frost glaze to-night the clear dew of his eyes,
And white ice-gauntlets glove his noble fine fair fingers o'er,
A warm dress is to him that lightning garb he ever wore,
The lightning of the soul, not skies.

Avran

Hugh marched forth to the fight—I grieved to see him so depart;
And lo! to-night he wanders frozen, rain-drenched, sad,
betrayed—
But the memory of the limewhite mansions his right hand hath laid
In ashes, warms the hero's heart!

James Clarence Mangan

THE NAMELESS ONE

Roll forth, my song, like the rushing river,
That sweeps along to the mighty sea;

God will inspire me while I deliver
        My soul to thee!

Tell thou the world, when my bones lie whitening
    Amid the last homes of youth and eld,
That there was once one whose blood ran lightning
        No eye beheld.

Tell how his boyhood was one drear night-hour,
    How shone for him, through its griefs and gloom,
No star of all heaven sends to light our
        Path to the tomb.

Roll on, my song, and to after ages
    Tell how, disdaining all earth can give,
He would have taught men, from wisdom's pages,
        The way to live.

And tell how trampled, derided, hated,
    And worn by weakness, disease, and wrong,
He fled for shelter to God, who mated
        His soul with song—

With song which alway, sublime or vapid,
    Flowed like a rill in the morning-beam,
Perchance not deep, but intense and rapid—
        A mountain stream.

Tell how this Nameless, condemned for years long
    To herd with demons from hell beneath,
Saw things that made him, with groans and tears, long
        For even death.

Go on to tell how, with genius wasted,
    Betrayed in friendship, befooled in love,
With spirit shipwrecked, and young hopes blasted,
        He still, still strove.

Till, spent with toil, dreeing death for others,
   And some whose hands should have wrought for him;
(If children live not for sires and mothers,)
       His mind grew dim.

And he fell far through that pit abysmal
   The gulf and grave of Maginn and Burns;
And pawned his soul for the devil's dismal
       Stock of returns.

But yet redeemed it in days of darkness,
   And shapes and signs of the final wrath,
When death, in hideous and ghastly starkness,
       Stood on his path.

And tell how now, amid wreck and sorrow,
   And want, and sickness, and houseless nights,
He bides in calmness the silent morrow,
       That no ray lights.

And lives he still, then? Yes! Old and hoary
   At thirty-nine, from despair and woe,
He lives enduring what future story
       Will never know.

Him grant a grave to, ye pitying noble,
   Deep in your bosoms! There let him dwell!
He, too, had tears for all souls in trouble,
       Here and in hell!

              James Clarence Mangan

SIBERIA

   In Siberia's wastes
     The Ice-wind's breath
  Woundeth like the toothèd steel.

Lost Siberia doth reveal
　Only blight and death.

Blight and death alone.
　No Summer shines.
Night is interblent with Day.
In Siberia's wastes alway
　The blood blackens, the heart pines.

In Siberia's wastes
　No tears are shed,
For they freeze within the brain.
Nought is felt but dullest pain,
　Pain acute, yet dead;

Pain as in a dream,
　When years go by
Funeral-paced, yet fugitive,
When man lives, and doth not live,
　Doth not live—nor die.

In Siberia's wastes
　Are sands and rocks.
Nothing blooms of green or soft,
But the snowpeaks rise aloft
　And the gaunt ice-blocks.

And the exile there
　Is one with those;
They are part, and he is part,
For the sands are in his heart,
　And the killing snows.

Therefore, in those wastes
　None curse the Czar.
Each man's tongue is cloven by
The North Blast, who heweth nigh
　With sharp scymitar.

And such doom he drees,
 Till hunger gnawn,
And cold-slain, he at length sinks there,
Yet scarce more a corpse than ere
 His last breath was drawn.

James Clarence Mangan

HY-BRASAIL

On the ocean that hollows the rocks where ye dwell,
A shadowy land has appeared, as they tell;
Men thought it a region of sunshine and rest,
And they called it *Hy-Brasail* the isle of the blest.
From year unto year on the ocean's blue rim,
The beautiful spectre showed lovely and dim;
The golden clouds curtained the deep where it lay,
And it looked like an Eden, away, far away!

A peasant who heard of the wonderful tale,
In the breeze of the Orient loosened his sail;
From Ara, the holy, he turned to the West,
For though Ara was holy, *Hy-Brasail* was blest.
He heard not the voices that called from the shore—
He heard not the rising wind's menacing roar;
Home, kindred, and safety, he left on that day,
And he sped to *Hy-Brasail*, away, far away!

Morn rose on the deep, and that shadowy isle,
O'er the faint rim of distance, reflected its smile;
Noon burned on the wave, and that shadowy shore
Seemed lovelily distant, and faint as before;
Lone evening came down on the wanderer's track,
And to Ara again he looked timidly back;
O! far on the verge of the ocean it lay,
Yet the isle of the blest was away, far away!

Rash dreamer, return! O ye winds of the main,
Bear him back to his own peaceful Ara again.
Rash fool! for a vision of fanciful bliss
To barter thy calm life of labour and peace.
The warning of reason was spoken in vain,
He never re-visited Ara again!
Night falls on the deep, amidst tempest and spray,
And he died on the waters, away, far away!

Gerald Griffin

MO CRAOIBHIN CNO
From the Irish

My heart is far from Liffey's tide
    And Dublin town;
It strays beyond the Southern side
    Of Cnoc-Maol-Donn,
Where Capa-chuinn hath woodlands green,
  Where Amhan-Mhor's waters flow,
Where dwell unsung, unsought, unseen
    Mo craoibhin cno,
Low clustering in her leafy screen,
    Mo craoibhin cno!

The high-bred dames of Dublin town
    Are rich and fair,
With wavy plume and silken gown,
    And stately air;
Can plumes compare thy dark brown hair?
  Can silks thy neck of snow?
Or measur'd pace thine artless grace?
    Mo craoibhin cno,
When harebells scarcely show thy trace,
    Mo craoibhin cno!

I've heard the songs by Liffey's wave
      That maidens sung—
They sung their land the Saxon's slave,
      In Saxon tongue—
O! bring me here that Gaelic dear
    Which cursed the Saxon foe,
When thou didst charm my raptured ear,
      Mo craoibhin cno!
And none but God's good angels near,
      Mo craoibhin cno!

I've wandered by the rolling Lee!
      And Lene's green bowers—
I've seen the Shannon's wide-spread sea
      And Limerick's towers—
And Liffey's tide, where halls of pride
    Frown o'er the flood below;
My wild heart strays to Amhan-mhor's side,
      Mo craoibhin cno!
With love and thee for aye to bide,
      Mo craoibhin cno!

                Edward Walsh

MAIRGRÉAD NI CHEALLEADH

At the dance in the village thy white foot was fleetest;
Thy voice in the concert of maidens was sweetest;
The swell of thy white breast made rich lovers follow;
And thy raven hair bound them, young Mairgréad ni Chealleadh.

Thy neck was, lost maid, than the *ceanabhan* whiter,
And the glow of thy cheek than the *monadan* brighter;
But death's chain hath bound thee, thine eye's glazed and
    hollow,
That shone like a sunburst, young Mairgréad ni Chealleadh.

No more shall mine ear drink thy melody swelling;
Nor thy beamy eye brighten the outlaw's dark dwelling;
Or thy soft heaving bosom my destiny hallow,
When thine arms twine around me, young Mairgréad ni
    Chealleadh.

The moss couch I brought thee to-day from the mountain,
Has drank the last drop of thy young heart's red fountain—
For this good scian beside me stuck deep and run hollow
In thy bosom of treason, young Mairgréad ni Chealleadh.

With strings of rich pearls thy white neck was laden,
And thy fingers with spoils of the Sassanach maiden:
Such rich silks enrob'd not the proud dames of Mallow—
Such pure gold they wore not as Mairgréad ni Chealleadh.

Alas! that my loved one her outlaw would injure—
Alas! that he e'er proved her treason's avenger!
That this right hand should make thee a bed cold and hollow,
When in Death's sleep it laid thee, Young Mairgréad ni
    Chealleadh!

And while to this lone cave my deep grief I'm venting,
The Saxon's keen bandog my footstep is scenting,
But true men await me afar in Duhallow,
Farewell, cave of slaughter, and Mairgréad ni Chealleadh.

Edward Walsh

FROM THE COLD SOD THAT'S O'ER YOU
From the Irish

From the cold sod that's o'er you
    I never shall sever;
Were my hands twined in yours, Love,
    I'd hold them for ever.

My fondest, my fairest,
　　We may now sleep together!
I've the cold earth's damp odour,
　　And I'm worn from the weather.

This heart filled with fondness
　　Is wounded and weary;
A dark gulf beneath it
　　Yawns jet-black and dreary.
When death comes, a victor,
　　In mercy to greet me,
On the wings of the whirlwind
　　In the wild wastes you'll meet me.

When the folk of my household
　　Suppose I am sleeping,
On your cold grave till morning
　　The lone watch I'm keeping.
My grief to the night wind
　　For the mild maid to render,
Who was my betrothed
　　Since infancy tender.

Remember the lone night
　　I last spent with you, Love,
Beneath the dark sloe-tree
　　When the icy wind blew, Love.
High praise to thy Saviour
　　No sin-stain had found you,
That your virginal glory
　　Shines brightly around you.

The priests and the friars
　　Are ceaselessly chiding,
That I love a young maiden
　　In life not abiding.

O! I'd shelter and shield you
   If wild storms were swelling!
And O, my wrecked hope,
   That the cold earth's your dwelling.

Edward Walsh

THE FAIRY NURSE

Sweet babe! a golden cradle holds thee,
And soft the snow-white fleece enfolds thee;
In airy bower I'll watch thy sleeping,
Where branchy trees to the breeze are sweeping.
      Shuheen sho, lulo lo

When mothers languish broken-hearted,
When young wives are from husbands parted,
Ah! little think the keeners lonely,
They weep some time-worn fairy only.
      Shuheen sho, lulo lo!

Within our magic halls of brightness,
Trips many a foot of snowy whiteness;
Stolen maidens, queens of fairy—
And kings and chiefs a sluagh shee airy.
      Shuheen sho, lulo lo!

Rest thee, babe! I love thee dearly,
And as thy mortal mother nearly;
Ours is the swiftest steed and proudest,
That moves where the tramp of the host is loudest.
      Shuheen sho, lulo lo!

Rest thee, babe! for soon thy slumbers
Shall flee at the magic koelshie's numbers;

In airy bower I'll watch thy sleeping,
Where branchy trees to the breeze are sweeping.
Shuheen sho, lulo lo!

Edward Walsh

A CUISLE GEAL MO CHROIDHE

The long, long wished-for hour has come,
    Yet come, astor, in vain;
And left thee but the wailing hum
    Of sorrow and of pain:
My light of life, my lonely love!
    Thy portion sure must be
Man's scorn below, God's wrath above—
    A cuisle geal mo chroidhe!

I've given thee manhood's early prime,
    And manhood's teeming years;
I've blessed thee in my merriest time,
    And shed with thee my tears;
And, mother, though thou cast away
    The child who'd die for thee,
My fondest wishes still should pray
    For cuisle geal mo chroidhe!

For thee I've tracked the mountain's sides,
    And slept within the brake,
More lonely than the swan that glides
    O'er Lua's fairy lake.
The rich have spurned me from their door,
    Because I'd make thee free;
Yet still I love thee more and more,
    A cuisle geal mo chroidhe!

I've run the Outlaw's brief career,
    And borne his load of ill;

His rocky couch—his dreamy fear—
   With fixed, sustaining will;
And should his last dark chance befall,
   Even that shall welcome be;
In Death I'd love thee best of all,
   A cuisle geal mo chroidhe!

'Twas prayed for thee the world around,
   'Twas hoped for thee by all,
That with one gallant sunward bound
   Thou'dst burst long ages' thrall;
Thy faith was tried, alas! and those
   Who'd peril all for thee
Were curs'd and branded as thy foes,
   A cuisle geal mo chroidhe!

What fate is thine, unhappy Isle,
   When even the trusted few
Would pay thee back with hate and guile,
   When most they should be true!
'Twas not my strength or spirit failed
   Or those who'd die for thee;
Who loved thee truly have not failed,
   A cuisle geal mo chroidhe!

              Michael Doheny

LAMENT OF THE IRISH EMIGRANT

I'm sittin' on the stile, Mary,
   Where we sat side by side,
On a bright May mornin', long ago,
   When first you were my bride:
The corn was springin' fresh and green,
   And the lark sang loud and high—

And the red was on your lip, Mary,
    And the love-light in your eye.

The *place* is little changed, Mary,
    The day is bright as then,
The lark's loud song is in my ear,
    And the corn is green again;
But I miss the soft clasp of your hand,
    And your breath, warm on my cheek;
And I still keep list'nin' for the words
    You never more will speak.

'Tis but a step down yonder lane,
    And the little church stands near—
The church where we were wed, Mary,
    I see the spire from here.
But the graveyard lies between, Mary,
    And my step might break your rest—
For I've laid you, darling! down to sleep,
    With your baby on your breast.

I'm very lonely now, Mary,
    For the poor make no new friends;
But, O! they love the better still,
    The few our Father sends!
And you were all I had, Mary,
    My blessin' and my pride!
There's nothin' left to care for now,
    Since my poor Mary died.

Yours was the good, brave heart, Mary,
    That still kept hoping on,
When the trust in God had left my soul,
    And my arm's young strength was gone;
There was comfort even on your lip,
    And the kind look on your brow—

I bless you, Mary, for that same,
　　Though you cannot hear me now.

I thank you for the patient smile
　　When your heart was fit to break,
When the hunger pain was gnawin' there,
　　And you hid it for my sake;
I bless you for the pleasant word,
　　When your heart was sad and sore—
O! I'm thankful you are gone, Mary,
　　Where grief can't reach you more!

I'm biddin' you a long farewell,
　　My Mary—kind and true!
But I'll not forget you, darling,
　　In the land I'm goin' to:
They say there's bread and work for all,
　　And the sun shines always there—
But I'll not forget old Ireland,
　　Were it fifty times as fair!

And often in those grand old woods
　　I'll sit and shut my eyes,
And my heart will travel back again
　　To the place where Mary lies;
And I'll think I see the little stile
　　Where we sat side by side,
And the springin' corn, and the bright May morn,
　　When first you were my bride.

Lady Dufferin

THE WELSHMEN OF TIRAWLEY

Scorney Bwee, the Barretts' bailiff, lewd and lame,
To lift the Lynott's taxes when he came,

Rudely drew a young maid to him!
Then the Lynotts rose and slew him,
And in Tubber-na-Scorney threw him—
   Small your blame,
   Sons of Lynott!
Sing the vengeance of the Welshmen of Tirawley.

Then the Barretts to the Lynotts gave a choice,
Saying, 'Hear, ye murderous brood, men and boys,
Choose ye now, without delay,
Will ye lose your eyesight, say,
Or your manhoods, here to-day?
   Sad your choice,
   Sons of Lynott!
Sing the vengeance of the Welshmen of Tirawley.

Then the little boys of the Lynotts, weeping, said,
'Only leave us our eyesight in our head.'
But the bearded Lynotts then
Quickly answered back again,
'Take our eyes, but leave us men,
   Alive or dead,
   Sons of Wattin!'
Sing the vengeance of the Welshmen of Tirawley.

So the Barretts with sewing-needles sharp and smooth,
Let the light out of the eyes of every youth,
And of every bearded man,
Of the broken Lynott clan;
Then their darkened faces wan
   Turning south
   To the river—
Sing the vengeance of the Welshmen of Tirawley.

O'er the slippery stepping-stones of Clochan-na-n'all
They drove them, laughing loud at every fall,

As their wandering footsteps dark
Failed to reach the slippery mark,
And the swift stream swallowed stark,
      One and all
      As they stumbled—
From the vengeance of the Welshmen of Tirawley.

Of all the blinded Lynotts one alone
Walk'd erect from stepping-stone to stone:
So back again they brought you,
And a second time they wrought you
With their needles; but never got you
      Once to groan,
      Emon Lynott,
For the vengeance of the Welshmen of Tirawley.

But with prompt-projected footsteps sure as ever,
Emon Lynott again cross'd the river.
Though Duvowen was rising fast,
And the shaking stones o'ercast
By cold floods boiling past;
      Yet you never,
      Emon Lynott,
Faltered once before your foemen of Tirawley.

But, turning on Ballintubber bank, you stood,
And the Barretts thus bespoke o'er the flood—
'O, ye foolish sons of Wattin,
Small amends are these you've gotten,
For, while Scorna Boy lies rotten,
      I am good
      For vengeance!'
Sing the vengeance of the Welshmen of Tirawley.

'For 'tis neither in eye nor eyesight that a man
Bears the fortunes of himself and his clan,

But in the manly mind,
These darken'd orbs behind,
That your needles could never find
            Though they ran
            Through my heart-strings!'
Sing the vengeance of the Welshmen of Tirawley.

'But, little your women's needles do I reck;
For the night from heaven never fell so black,
But Tirawley, and abroad
From the Moy to Cuan-an-fod,
I could walk it every sod,
            Path and track,
            Ford and togher,
Seeking vengeance on you, Barretts of Tirawley!'

'The night when Dathy O'Dowda broke your camp,
What Barrett among you was it held the lamp—
Showed the way to those two feet,
When through wintry wind and sleet,
I guided your blind retreat
            In the swamp
            Of Beäl-an-asa?
O ye vengeance-destined ingrates of Tirawley!'

So leaving loud-shriek-echoing Garranard,
The Lynott like a red dog hunted hard,
With his wife and children seven,
'Mong the beasts and fowls of heaven
In the hollows of Glen Nephin,
            Light-debarred,
            Made his dwelling,
Planning vengeance on the Barretts of Tirawley.

And ere the bright-orb'd year its course had run,
On his brown round-knotted knee he nursed a son,

A child of light, with eyes
As clear as are the skies
In summer, when sunrise
   Has begun;
   So the Lynott
Nursed his vengeance on the Barretts of Tirawley.

And, as ever the bright boy grew in strength and size,
Made him perfect in each manly exercise,
The salmon in the flood,
The dun deer in the wood,
The eagle in the cloud
   To surprise
   On Ben Nephin,
Far above the foggy fields of Tirawley.

With the yellow-knotted spear-shaft, with the bow,
With the steel, prompt to deal shot and blow,
He taught him from year to year
And train'd him, without a peer,
For a perfect cavalier,
   Hoping so—
   Far his forethought—
For vengeance on the Barretts of Tirawley.

And, when mounted on his proud-bounding steed,
Emon Oge sat a cavalier indeed;
Like the ear upon the wheat
When winds in Autumn beat
On the bending stems, his seat;
   And the speed
   Of his courser
Was the wind from Barna-na-gee o'er Tirawley!

Now when fifteen sunny summers thus were spent,
(He perfected in all accomplishment)—

The Lynott said, 'My child,
We are over long exiled
From mankind in this wild—
   —Time we went
   Through the mountain
To the countries lying over-against Tirawley.'

So, out over mountain-moors, and mosses brown,
And green steam-gathering vales, they journey'd down:
Till, shining like a star,
Through the dusky gleams afar,
The bailey of Castlebar,
   And the town
   Of MacWilliam
Rose bright before the wanderers of Tirawley.

'Look southward, my boy, and tell me as we go,
What see'st thou by the loch-head below?'
'O, a stone-house strong and great,
And a horse-host at the gate,
And a captain in armour of plate—
   Grand the show!
   Great the glancing!
High the heroes of this land below Tirawley.

'And a beautiful Bantierna by his side,
Yellow gold on all her gown-sleeves wide;
And in her hand a pearl
Of a young, little, fair-haired girl.'
Said the Lynott, 'It is the Earl!
   Let us ride
   To his presence.'
And before him came the exiles of Tirawley.

'God save thee, MacWilliam,' the Lynott thus began;
'God save all here besides of this clan;

For gossips dear to me
Are all in company—
For in these four bones ye see
> A kindly man
> Of the Britons—
Emon Lynott of Garranard of Tirawley.

'And hither, as kindly gossip-law allows,
I come to claim a scion of thy house
To foster; for thy race,
Since William Conquer's days,
Have ever been wont to place,
> With some spouse
> Of a Briton,
A MacWilliam Oge, to foster in Tirawley.

'And to show thee in what sort our youth are taught
I have hither to thy home of valour brought
This one son of my age,
For a sample and a pledge
For the equal tutelage,
> In right thought,
> Word, and action,
Of whatever son ye give into Tirawley.'

When MacWilliam beheld the brave boy ride and run,
Saw the spear-shaft from his white shoulder spun—
With a sigh, and with a smile,
He said,—'I would give the spoil
Of a county, that Tibbot Moyle,
> My own son,
> Were accomplish'd
Like this branch of the kindly Britons of Tirawley.'

When the Lady MacWilliam she heard him speak,
And saw the ruddy roses on his cheek,

She said, 'I would give a purse
Of red gold to the nurse
That would rear my Tibbot no worse;
      But I seek
      Hitherto vainly—
Heaven grant that I now have found her in Tirawley!'

So they said to the Lynott, 'Here, take our bird!
And as pledge for the keeping of thy word,
Let this scion here remain
Till thou comest back again:
Meanwhile the fitting train
      Of a lord
      Shall attend thee
With the lordly heir of Connaught into Tirawley.'

So back to strong-throng-gathering Garranard,
Like a lord of the country with his guard,
Came the Lynott, before them all,
Once again over Clochan-na-n'all
Steady and striding, erect and tall,
      And his ward
      On his shoulders
To the wonder of the Welshmen of Tirawley.

Then a diligent foster-father you would deem
The Lynott, teaching Tibbot, by mead and stream,
To cast the spear, to ride,
To stem the rushing tide,
With what feats of body beside,
      Might beseem
      A MacWilliam,
Fostered free among the Welshmen of Tirawley.

But the lesson of hell he taught him in heart and mind,
For to what desire soever he inclined,

Of anger, lust, or pride,
He had it gratified,
Till he ranged the circle wide
            Of a blind
            Self-indulgence,
Ere he came to youthful manhood in Tirawley.

Then, even as when a hunter slips a hound,
Lynott loosed him—God's leashes all unbound—
In the pride of power and station,
And the strength of youthful passion,
On the daughters of thy nation,
            All around,
            Wattin Barrett!
O! the vengeance of the Welshmen of Tirawley!

Bitter grief and burning anger, rage and shame,
Filled the houses of the Barretts where'er he came;
Till the young men of the Back,
Drew by night upon his track,
And slew him at Cornassack.
            Small your blame,
            Sons of Wattin!
Sing the vengeance of the Welshmen of Tirawley.

Said the Lynott, 'The day of my vengeance is drawing near,
The day for which, through many a long dark year,
I have toiled through grief and sin—
Call ye now the Brehons in,
And let the plea begin
            Over the bier
            Of MacWilliam,
For an eric upon the Barretts of Tirawley!'

Then the Brehons to MacWilliam Burke decreed
An eric upon Clan Barrett for the deed;

And the Lynott's share of the fine,
As foster-father, was nine
Ploughlands and nine score kine;
          But no need
          Had the Lynott,
Neither care, for land or cattle in Tirawley.

But rising, while all sat silent on the spot,
He said, 'The law says—doth it not?—
If the foster-sire elect
His portion to reject,
He may then the right exact
          To applot
          The short eric.'
''Tis the law,' replied the Brehons of Tirawley.

Said the Lynott, 'I once before had a choice
Proposed me, wherein law had little voice;
But now I choose, and say,
As lawfully I may,
I applot the mulct to-day;
          So rejoice
          In your ploughlands
And your cattle which I renounce throughout Tirawley.

'And thus I applot the mulct: I divide
The land throughout Clan Barrett on every side
Equally, that no place
May be without the face
Of a foe of Wattin's race—
          That the pride
          Of the Barretts
May be humbled hence for ever throughout Tirawley.

'I adjudge a seat in every Barrett's hall
To MacWilliam: in every stable I give a stall

To MacWilliam: and, beside,
Whenever a Burke shall ride
Through Tirawley, I provide
            At his call
            Needful grooming,
Without charge from any Brughaidh of Tirawley.

'Thus lawfully I avenge me for the throes
Ye lawlessly caused me and caused those
Unhappy shame-faced ones
Who, their mothers expected once,
Would have been the sires of sons—
            O'er whose woes
            Often weeping,
I have groaned in my exile from Tirawley.

'I demand not of you your manhoods; but I take—
For the Burkes will take it—your Freedom! for the sake
Of which all manhood's given
And all good under heaven,
And, without which, better even
            You should make
            Yourselves barren,
Than see your children slaves throughout Tirawley!

'Neither take I your eyesight from you; as you took
Mine and ours: I would have you daily look
On one another's eyes
When the strangers tyrannize
By your hearths, and blushes arise,
            That ye brook
            Without vengeance
The insults of troops of Tibbots throughout Tirawley!

'The vengeance I designed, now is done,
And the days of me and mine nearly run—

For, for this, I have broken faith,
Teaching him who lies beneath
This pall, to merit death;
   And my son
   To his father
Stands pledged for other teaching in Tirawley.'

Said MacWilliam—'Father and son, hang them high!'
And the Lynott they hang'd speedily;
But across the salt water,
To Scotland, with the daughter
Of MacWilliam—well you got her!—
   Did you fly
   Edmund Lindsay,
The gentlest of all the Welshmen of Tirawley!

'Tis thus the ancient Ollaves of Erin tell
How, through lewdness and revenge, it befell
That the sons of William Conquer
Came over the sons of Wattin,
Throughout all the bounds and borders
Of the lands of Auley Mac Fiachra;
Till the Saxon Oliver Cromwell,
And his valiant, Bible-guided,
Free heretics of Clan London
Coming in, in their succession,
Rooted out both Burke and Barrett,
And in their empty places
New stems of freedom planted,
With many a goodly sapling
Of manliness and virtue;
Which while their children cherish,
Kindly Irish of the Irish,
Neither Saxons nor Italians,

May the mighty God of Freedom
    Speed them well,
    Never taking
Further vengeance on his people of Tirawley.

               Sir Samuel Ferguson

AIDEEN'S GRAVE

They heaved the stone; they heap'd the cairn.
    Said Ossian, 'In a queenly grave
We leave her, 'mong her fields of fern,
    Between the cliff and wave.

'The cliff behind stands clear and bare,
    And bare, above, the heathery steep
Scales the clear heaven's expanse, to where
    The Danaan Druids sleep.

'And all the sands that, left and right,
    The grassy isthmus-ridge confine,
In yellow bars lie bare and bright
    Among the sparkling brine.

'A clear pure air pervades the scene,
    In loneliness and awe secure;
Meet spot to sepulchre a Queen
    Who in her life was pure.

'Here, far from camp and chase removed,
    Apart in Nature's quiet room,
The music that alive she loved
    Shall cheer her in the tomb.

'The humming of the noontide bees,
    The lark's loud carol all day long,
And, borne on evening's salted breeze,
    The clanking sea-bird's song,

'Shall round her airy chamber float,
    And with the whispering winds and streams,
Attune to Nature's tenderest note
    The tenor of her dreams.

'And oft, at tranquil eve's decline,
    When full tides lip the Old Green Plain,
The lowing of Moynalty's kine
    Shall round her breathe again.

'In sweet remembrance of the days
    When, duteous, in the lowly vale,
Unconscious of my Oscar's gaze,
    She fill'd the fragrant pail,

'And, duteous, from the running brook
    Drew water for the bath; nor deem'd
A king did on her labour look,
    And she a fairy seem'd.

'But when the wintry frosts begin,
    And in their long-drawn, lofty flight,
The wild geese with their airy din
    Distend the ear of night,

'And when the fierce De Danaan ghosts
    At midnight from their peak come down,
When all around the enchanted coasts
    Despairing strangers drown;

'When, mingling with the wreckful wail,
    From low Clontarf's wave-trampled floor
Comes booming up the burthen'd gale
    The angry Sand-Bull's roar;

'Or, angrier than the sea, the shout
    Of Erin's hosts in wrath combined,

When Terror heads Oppression's rout,
   And Freedom cheers behind:—

'Then o'er our lady's placid dream,
   Where safe from storms she sleeps, may steal
Such joy as will not misbeseem
   A Queen of men to feel:

'Such thrill of free, defiant pride,
   As rapt her in her battle-car
At Gavra, when by Oscar's side
   She rode the ridge of war,

'Exulting, down the shouting troops,
   And through the thick confronting kings,
With hands on all their javelin loops
   And shafts on all their strings;

'E'er closed the inseparable crowds,
   No more to part for me, and show,
As bursts the sun through scattering clouds,
   My Oscar issuing so.

'No more, dispelling battle's gloom,
   Shall son for me from fight return;
The great green rath's ten-acred tomb
   Lies heavy on his urn.

'A cup of bodkin-pencill'd clay
   Holds Oscar; mighty heart and limb
One handful now of ashes grey:
   And she has died for him.

'And here, hard by her natal bower
   On lone Ben Edar's side, we strive
With lifted rock and sign of power
   To keep her name alive.

'That while from circling year to year,
    Her Ogham-letter'd stone is seen,
The Gael shall say, "Our Fenians here
    Entombed their loved Aideen."

'The Ogham from her pillar-stone
    In tract of time will wear away;
Her name at last be only known
    In Ossian's echo'd lay.

'The long-forgotten lay I sing
    May only ages hence revive,
(As eagle with a wounded wing
    To soar again might strive,)

'Imperfect, in an alien speech,
    When, wandering here, some child of chance
Through pangs of keen delight shall reach
    The gift of utterance,—

'To speak the air, the sky to speak,
    The freshness of the hill to tell,
Who, roaming bare Ben Edar's peak
    And Aideen's briary dell,

'And gazing on the Cromlech vast,
    And on the mountain and the sea,
Shall catch communion with the past
    And mix himself with me.

'Child of the Future's doubtful night,
    Whate'er your speech, whoe'er your sires,
Sing while you may with frank delight
    The song your hour inspires.

'Sing while you may, nor grieve to know
    The song you sing shall also die;

Atharna's lay has perish'd so,
   Though once it thrill'd this sky,

'Above us, from his rocky chair,
   There, where Ben Edar's landward crest
O'er eastern Bregia bends, to where
   Dun Almon crowns the west:

'And all that felt the fretted air
   Throughout the song-distempered clime,
Did droop, till suppliant Leinster's prayer
   Appeased the vengeful rhyme.

'Ah me, or e'er the hour arrive
   Shall bid my long-forgotten tones,
Unknown One, on your lips revive
   Here by these moss-grown stones,

'What change shall o'er the scene have crossed;
   What conquering lords anew have come
What lore-arm'd, mightier Druid host
   From Gaul or distant Rome!

'What arts of death, what ways of life,
   What creeds unknown to bard or seer,
Shall round your careless steps be rife,
   Who pause and ponder here;

'And, haply, where yon curlew calls
   Athwart the marsh, 'mid groves and bowers,
See rise some mighty chieftain's halls
   With unimagined towers:

'And baying hounds, and coursers bright,
   And burnish'd cars of dazzling sheen,
With courtly train of dame and knight,
   Where now the fern is green.

'Or, by yon prostrate altar-stone
    May kneel, perchance, and, free from blame,
New holy men with rites unknown
    New names of God proclaim.

'Let change as may the Name of Awe,
    Let right surcease and altar pall,
The same One God remains, a law
    For ever and for all.

'Let change as may the face of earth,
    Let alter all the social frame,
For mortal men the warp of birth
    And death are still the same.

'And still, as life and time wear on,
    The children of the waning days,
(Though strength be from their shoulders gone
    To lift the loads we raise,)

'Shall weep to do the burial rites
    Of lost ones loved; and fondly found,
In shadow of the gathering nights,
    The monumental mound.

'Farewell! the strength of men is worn:
    The night approaches dark and chill:
Sleep, till perchance an endless morn
    Descend the glittering hill.'

Of Oscar and Aideen bereft,
    So Ossian's song. The Fenians sped
Three mighty shouts to heaven; and left
    Ben Edar to the dead.

                    Sir Samuel Ferguson

DEIRDRE'S LAMENT FOR THE SONS OF USNACH
From the Irish

The lions of the hill are gone,
And I am left alone—alone—
Dig the grave both wide and deep,
For I am sick, and fain would sleep!

The falcons of the wood are flown,
And I am left alone—alone—
Dig the grave both deep and wide,
And let us slumber side by side.

The dragons of the rock are sleeping,
Sleep that wakes not for our weeping—
Dig the grave, and make it ready,
Lay me on my true-love's body.

Lay their spears and bucklers bright
By the warriors' sides aright;
Many a day the three before me
On their linkèd bucklers bore me.

Lay upon the low grave floor,
'Neath each head, the blue claymore;
Many a time the noble three
Reddened these blue blades for me.

Lay the collars, as is meet,
Of their greyhounds at their feet;
Many a time for me have they
Brought the tall red deer to bay.

In the falcon's jesses throw,
Hook and arrow, line and bow;
Never again, by stream or plain,
Shall the gentle woodsmen go.

Sweet companions, ye were ever—
Harsh to me, your sister, never;
Woods and wilds, and misty valleys,
Were with you as good's a palace.

O, to hear my true-love singing,
Sweet as sound of trumpets ringing;
Like the sway of ocean swelling
Rolled his deep voice round our dwelling.

O! to hear the echoes pealing
Round our green and fairy sheeling,
When the three, with soaring chorus,
Passed the silent skylark o'er us.

Echo now, sleep, morn and even—
Lark alone enchant the heaven!
Ardan's lips are scant of breath,
Neesa's tongue is cold in death.

Stag, exult on glen and mountain—
Salmon, leap from loch to fountain—
Heron, in the free air warm ye—
Usnach's sons no more will harm ye!

Erin's stay no more you are,
Rulers of the ridge of war;
Never more 'twill be your fate
To keep the beam of battle straight!

Woe is me! by fraud and wrong,
Traitors false and tyrants strong,
Fell Clan Usnach, bought and sold,
For Barach's feast and Conor's gold!

Woe to Eman, roof and wall!
Woe to Red Branch, hearth and hall!—

Tenfold woe and black dishonour
To the foul and false Clan Conor!

Dig the grave both wide and deep,
Sick I am, and fain would sleep!
Dig the grave and make it ready,
Lay me on my true-love's body.

Sir Samuel Ferguson

THE FAIR HILLS OF IRELAND
From the Irish

A plenteous place is Ireland for hospitable cheer,
Uileacan dubh O!
Where the wholesome fruit is bursting from the yellow barley
ear;
Uileacan dubh O!
There is honey in the trees where her misty vales expand,
And her forest paths in summer are by falling waters fanned;
There is dew at high noontide there, and springs i' the yellow
sand,
On the fair hills of holy Ireland.

Curled he is and ringleted, and plaited to the knee,
Uileacan dubh O!
Each captain who comes sailing across the Irish sea;
Uileacan dubh O!
And I will make my journey, if life and health but stand,
Unto that pleasant country, that fresh and fragrant strand,
And leave your boasted braveries, your wealth and high
command,
For the fair hills of holy Ireland.

Large and profitable are the stacks upon the ground;
Uileacan dubh O!

The butter and the cream do wondrously abound,
>> *Uileacan dubh O!*
The cresses on the water and the sorrels are at hand,
And the cuckoo's calling daily his note of music bland,
And the bold thrush sings so bravely his song i' the forest grand,
> On the fair hills of holy Ireland.

Sir Samuel Ferguson

LAMENT OVER THE RUINS OF THE ABBEY OF TIMOLEAGUE
From the Irish

Lone and weary as I wander'd by the bleak shore of the sea,
Meditating and reflecting on the world's hard destiny,
Forth the moon and stars 'gan glimmer, in the quiet tide
> beneath,
For on slumbering spring and blossom breathed not out of
> heaven a breath.

On I went in sad dejection, careless where my footsteps bore,
Till a ruined church before me opened wide its ancient door,—
Till I stood before the portals, where of old were wont to be,
For the blind, the halt, and leper, alms and hospitality.

Still the ancient seat was standing, built against the buttress grey,
Where the clergy used to welcome weary trav'llers on their way;
There I sat me down in sadness, 'neath my cheek I placed my
> hand,
Till the tears fell hot and briny down upon the grassy land.

There, I said in woful sorrow, weeping bitterly the while,
Was a time when joy and gladness reigned within this ruined
> pile;—

Was a time when bells were tinkling, clergy preaching peace
    abroad,
Psalms a-singing, music ringing praises to the mighty God.

Empty aisle, deserted chancel, tower tottering to your fall,
Many a storm since then has beaten on the grey head of your
    wall!
Many a bitter storm and tempest has your roof-tree turned away,
Since you first were formed a temple to the Lord of night and
    day.

Holy house of ivied gables, that were once the country's boast,
Houseless now in weary wandering are you scattered, saintly
    host;
Lone you are to-day, and dismal,—joyful psalms no more are
    heard,
Where, within your choir, her vesper screeches the cat-headed
    bird.

Ivy from your eaves is growing, nettles round your green
    hearth-stone,
Foxes howl, where, in your corners, dropping waters make their
    moan.
Where the lark to early matins used your clergy forth to call,
There, alas! no tongue is stirring, save the daw's upon the wall.

Refectory cold and empty, dormitory bleak and bare,
Where are now your pious uses, simple bed and frugal fare?
Gone your abbot, rule and order, broken down your altar stones;
Nought see I beneath your shelter, save a heap of clayey bones.

O! the hardship, O! the hatred, tyranny, and cruel war,
Persecution and oppression, that have left you as you are!
I myself once also prosper'd;—mine is, too, an alter'd plight;
Trouble, care, and age have left me good for nought but grief
    to-night.

Gone my motion and my vigour—gone the use of eye and ear,
At my feet lie friends and children, powerless and corrupting
   here;
Woe is written on my visage, in a nut my heart could lie—
Death's deliverance were welcome—Father, let the old man die.

Sir Samuel Ferguson

THE FAIRY WELL OF LAGNANAY

Mournfully, sing mournfully—
   'O listen, Ellen, sister dear:
Is there no help at all for me,
   But only ceaseless sigh and tear?
   Why did not he who left me here,
With stolen hope steal memory?
   O listen, Ellen, sister dear,
(Mournfully, sing mournfully)—
   I'll go away to Slemish hill,
I'll pluck the fairy hawthorn-tree,
   And let the spirits work their will;
   I care not if for good or ill,
So they but lay the memory
   Which all my heart is haunting still!
(Mournfully, sing mournfully)—
   The Fairies are a silent race,
And pale as lily flowers to see:
   I care not for a blanchèd face,
   Nor wandering in a dreaming place,
So I but banish memory:—
   I wish I were with Anna Grace!'
Mournfully, sing mournfully!

Hearken to my tale of woe—
   'Twas thus to weeping Ellen Con,

Her sister said in accents low,
    Her only sister, Una bawn:
    'Twas in their bed before the dawn,
And Ellen answered sad and slow,—
    'O Una, Una, be not drawn
(Hearken to my tale of woe)—
    To this unholy grief I pray,
Which makes me sick at heart to know,
    And I will help you if I may:
    —The Fairy Well of Lagnanay—
Lie nearer me, I tremble so,—
    Una, I've heard wise women say
(Hearken to my tale of woe)—
    That if before the dews arise,
True maiden in its icy flow
    With pure hand bathe her bosom thrice,
    Three lady-brackens pluck likewise,
And three times round the fountain go,
    She straight forgets her tears and sighs.'
Hearken to my tale of woe!

All, alas! and well-away!
    'O, sister Ellen, sister sweet,
Come with me to the hill I pray,
    And I will prove that blessed freet!'
    They rose with soft and silent feet,
They left their mother where she lay,
    Their mother and her care discreet,
(All, alas! and well-away!)
    And soon they reached the Fairy Well,
The mountain's eye, clear, cold, and grey,
    Wide open in the dreary fell:
    How long they stood 'twere vain to tell,
At last upon the point of day,
    Bawn Una bares her bosom's swell,

(All, alas! and well-away!)
   Thrice o'er her shrinking breasts she laves
The gliding glance that will not stay
   Of subtly-streaming fairy waves:—
   And now the charm three brackens craves,
She plucks them in their fring'd array:—
   Now round the well her fate she braves,
All, alas! and well-away!

Save us all from Fairy thrall!
   Ellen sees her face the rim
Twice and thrice, and that is all—
   Fount and hill and maiden swim
   All together melting dim!
'Una! Una!' thou may'st call,
   Sister sad! but lith or limb
(Save us all from Fairy thrall!)
   Never again of Una bawn,
Where now she walks in dreamy hall,
   Shall eyes of mortal look upon!
   O! can it be the guard was gone,
That better guard than shield or wall?
   Who knows on earth save Jurlagh Daune?
(Save us all from Fairy thrall!)
   Behold the banks are green and bare,
No pit is here wherein to fall:
   Aye—at the fount you well may stare,
   But nought save pebbles smooth is there,
And small straws twirling one and all.
   Hie thee home, and be thy prayer,
Save us all from Fairy thrall.

Sir Samuel Ferguson

ON THE DEATH OF THOMAS DAVIS

I walked through Ballinderry in the Spring-time,
    When the bud was on the tree;
And I said, in every fresh-ploughed field beholding
    The sowers striding free,
Scattering broad-cast forth the corn in golden plenty
    On the quick seed-clasping soil,
Even such, this day, among the fresh-stirred hearts of Erin,
    Thomas Davis, is thy toil!

I sat by Ballyshannon in the summer,
    And saw the salmon leap;
And I said, as I beheld the gallant creatures
    Spring glittering from the deep,
Through the spray, and through the prone heaps striving
        onward
    To the calm clear streams above,
So seekest thou they native founts of freedom, Thomas Davis,
    In thy brightness of strength and love!

I stood on Derrybawn in the Autumn,
    I heard the eagle call,
With a clangorous cry of wrath and lamentation
    That filled the wide mountain hall,
O'er the bare deserted place of his plundered eyrie;
    And I said, as he screamed and soared,
So callest thou, thou wrathful-soaring Thomas Davis,
    For a nation's rights restored!

And, alas! to think but now, and thou art lying,
    Dear Davis, dead at thy mother's knee;
And I, no mother near, on my own sick-bed,
    That face on earth shall never see:
I may lie and try to feel that I am not dreaming,
    I may lie and try to say 'Thy will be done'—

But a hundred such as I will never comfort Erin
    For the loss of the noble son!

Young husbandman of Erin's fruitful seed-time,
    In the fresh track of danger's plough!
Who will walk the heavy, toilsome, perilous furrow
    Girt with freedom's seed-sheets now?
Who will banish with the wholesome crop of knowledge
    The flaunting weed and the bitter thorn,
Now that thou thyself art but a seed for hopeful planting
    Against the resurrection morn?

Young salmon of the flood-time of freedom
    That swells round Erin's shore!
Thou wilt leap against their loud oppressive torrent
    Of bigotry and hate no more:
Drawn downward by their prone material instinct,
    Let them thunder on their rocks and foam—
Thou hast leapt, aspiring soul, to founts beyond their raging,
    Where troubled waters never come!

But I grieve not, eagle of the empty eyrie,
    That thy wrathful cry is still;
And that the songs alone of peaceful mourners
    Are heard to-day on Erin's hill;
Better far, if brothers' war be destined for us
    (God avert that horrid day I pray!)
That ere our hands be stained with slaughter fratricidal
    Thy warm heart should be cold in clay.

But my trust is strong in God, who made us brothers,
    That He will not suffer those right hands
Which thou hast joined in holier rites than wedlock,
    To draw opposing brands.
O, many a tuneful tongue that thou madest vocal
    Would lie cold and silent then;

And songless long once more, should often-widowed Erin
    Mourn the loss of her brave young men.

O, brave young men, my love, my pride, my promise,
    'Tis on you my hopes are set,
In manliness, in kindliness, in justice,
    To make Erin a nation yet:
Self-respecting, self-relying, self-advancing,
    In union or in severance, free and strong—
And if God grant this, then, under God, to Thomas Davis
    Let the greater praise belong.

Sir Samuel Ferguson

THE COUNTY OF MAYO
From the Irish of Thomas Lavelle

On the deck of Patrick Lynch's boat I sat in woful plight,
Through my sighing all the weary day, and weeping all the
    night;
Were it not that full of sorrow from my people forth I go,
By the blessed sun! 'tis royally I'd sing thy praise, Mayo!

When I dwelt at home in plenty, and my gold did much abound,
In the company of fair young maids the Spanish ale went
    round—
'Tis a bitter change from those gay days that now I'm forced to
    go,
And must leave my bones in Santa Cruz, far from my own Mayo.

They are altered girls in Irrul now; 'tis proud they're grown and
    high,
With their hair-bags and their top-knots, for I pass their buckles
    by—
But it's little now I heed their airs, for God will have it so,
That I must depart for foreign lands, and leave my sweet Mayo.

'Tis my grief that Patrick Loughlin is not Earl of Irrul still,
And that Brian Duff no longer rules as Lord upon the hill:
And that Colonel Hugh MacGrady should be lying dead and low,
And I sailing, sailing swiftly from the county of Mayo.

George Fox

THE WEDDING OF THE CLANS
A girl's babble

I go to knit two clans together;
   Our clan and this clan unseen of yore:—
Our clan fears nought! but I go, O whither?
   This day I go from my mother's door.

Thou, red-breast, singest the old song over,
   Though many a time thou hast sung it before;
They never sent thee to some strange new lover:—
   I sing a new song by my mother's door.

I stepped from my little room down by the ladder,
   The ladder that never so shook before;
I was sad last night; to-day I am sadder,
   Because I go from my mother's door.

The last snow melts upon bush and bramble;
   The gold bars shine on the forest's floor;
Shake not, thou leaf! it is I must tremble
   Because I go from my mother's door.

From a Spanish sailor a dagger I bought me;
   I trailed a rose-tree our grey bawn o'er;
The creed and my letters our old bard taught me;
   My days were sweet by my mother's door.

My little white goat that with raised feet huggest
   The oak stock, thy horns in the ivies frore,

Could I wrestle like thee—how the wreaths thou tuggest!—
   I never would move from my mother's door.

O weep no longer, my nurse and mother!
   My foster-sister, weep not so sore!
You cannot come with me, Ir, my brother—
   Alone I go from my mother's door.

Farewell, my wolf-hound that slew MacOwing
   As he caught me and far through the thickets bore:
My heifer, Alb, in the green vale lowing,
   My cygnet's nest upon Lorna's shore!

He has killed ten chiefs, this chief that plights me,
   His hand is like that of the giant Balor;
But I fear his kiss, and his beard affrights me,
   And the great stone dragon above his door.

Had I daughters nine, with me they should tarry;
   They should sing old songs; they should dance at my door;
They should grind at the quern;—no need to marry;
   O when will this marriage-day be o'er?

Had I buried, like Moirín, three mates already,
   I might say: 'Three husbands! then why not four?'
But my hand is cold and my foot unsteady,
   Because I never was married before!

Aubrey de Vere

THE LITTLE BLACK ROSE

The Little Black Rose shall be red at last;
   What made it black but the March wind dry,
And the tear of the widow that fell on it fast?
   It shall redden the hills when June is nigh.

The Silk of the Kine shall rest at last;
   What drove her forth but the dragon-fly?
In the golden vale she shall feed full fast,
   With her mild gold horn and her slow, dark eye.

The wounded wood-dove lies dead at last!
   The pine long bleeding, it shall not die!
This song is secret. Mine ear it passed
   In a wind o'er the plains at Athenry.

                Aubrey de Vere

SONG

She says: 'Poor Friend, you waste a treasure
   Which you can ne'er regain—
Time, health, and glory, for the pleasure
   Of toying with a chain.'
But then her voice so tender grows,
   So kind and so caressing;
Each murmur from her lips that flows
   Comes to me like a blessing.

Sometimes she says: 'Sweet Friend, I grieve you—
   Alas, it gives me pain!
What can I? Ah, might I relieve you,
   You ne'er had mourned in vain!'
And then her little hand she presses
   Upon her heart, and sighs;
While tears, whose source not yet she guesses,
   Grow larger in her eyes.

                Aubrey de Vere

THE BARD ETHELL
Ireland in the thirteenth century

I am Ethell, the son of Conn:
    Here I bide at the foot of the hill:
I am clansman to Brian, and servant to none:
    Whom I hated, I hate: whom I loved, I love
        still.
Blind am I. On milk I live,
    And meat, God sends it, on each Saint's Day;
Though Donald Mac Art—may he never thrive—
    Last Shrovetide drove half my kine away.

At the brown hill's base by the pale blue lake
    I dwell and see the things I saw:
The heron flap heavily up from the brake;
    The crow fly homeward with twig or straw
The wild duck a silver line in wake
    Cutting the calm mere to far Bunaw.
And the things that I heard, though deaf, I hear,
From the tower in the island the feastful cheer;
The horn from the wood; the plunge of the stag,
With the loud hounds after him down from
      the crag.
Sweet is the chase, but the battle is sweeter,
More healthy, more joyous, for true men meeter!

My hand is weak! it once was strong:
    My heart burns still with its ancient fire.
If any man smites me he does me wrong,
    For I was the bard of Brian Mac Guire.
If any man slay me—not unaware,
    By no chance blow, nor in wine and revel,
I have stored beforehand, a curse in my prayer
    For his kith and kindred; his deed is evil.

There never was king, and never will be,
In battle or banquet like Malachi!
The seers his reign had predicted long;
He honoured the bards, and gave gold for song.
If rebels arose, he put out their eyes;

If robbers plundered or burned the fanes,
He hung them in chaplets, like rosaries,

That others beholding might take more pains!
There was none to women more reverent-minded,

For he held his mother, and Mary, dear;
If any man wronged them, that man he blinded,

Or straight amerced him of hand or ear.
There was none who founded more convents—none;

In his palace the old and poor were fed;
The orphan might walk, or the widow's son,

Without groom or page to his throne or bed.
In his council he mused, with great brows divine,
And eyes like the eyes of the musing kine,
Upholding a sceptre o'er which men said,
Seven spirits of wisdom like fire-tongues played.
He drained ten lakes, and he built ten bridges;

He bought a gold book for a thousand cows;
He slew ten princes who brake their pledges;

With the bribed and the base he scorned to carouse.
He was sweet and awful; through all his reign
God gave great harvests to vale and plain;
From his nurse's milk he was kind and brave;
And when he went down to his well-wept grave,
Through the triumph of penance his soul arose
To God and the saints. Not so his foes.

The King that came after, ah woe, woe, woe!
He doubted his friend, and he trusted his foe,
He bought and he sold: his kingdom old

He pledged and pawned, to avenge a spite:

No Bard or prophet his birth foretold:
    He was guarded and warded both day and night:
He counselled with fools and had boors at his feast:
He was cruel to Christian and kind to beast:
Men smiled when they talked of him far o'er the wave:
Well paid were the mourners that wept at his grave.
God plagued for his sake his people sore:
    They sinned; for the people should watch and pray,
That their prayers like angels at window and door,
    May keep from the King the bad thought away!

The sun has risen: on lip and brow,
    He greets me—I feel it—with golden wand:
Ah, bright-faced Norna! I see thee now:
    Where first I saw thee I see thee stand!
From the trellis the girl looked down on me:
    Her maidens stood near; it was late in spring;
The grey priest laughed, as she cried in glee,
    'Good Bard, a song in my honour sing.'
I sang her praise in a loud-voiced hymn,
To God who had fashioned her face and limb,
For the praise of the clan, and the land's behoof:
So she flung me a flower from the trellis roof.
Ere long I saw her the hill descending,
    O'er the lake the May morning rose moist and slow,
She prayed me, her smile with the sweet voice blending,
    To teach her all that a woman should know.
Panting she stood; she was out of breath;
    The wave of her little breast was shaking;
From eyes still childish, and dark as death,
    Came womanhood's dawn through a dew-cloud breaking.
Norna was never long time the same;
    By a spirit so strong was her slight form moulded,
The curves swelled out from the flower-like frame
    In joy; in grief to a bud she folded:

As she listened, her eyes grew bright and large,
Like springs rain-fed that dilate their marge.
So I taught her the hymn of Patrick the Apostle,
    And the marvels of Bridget and Columbkille;
Ere long she sang like the lark or the throstle,
    Sang the deeds of the servants of God's high will:
I told her of Brendan, who found afar
Another world 'neath the western star;
Of our three great bishops in Lindisfarne isle;
Of St. Fursey the wondrous, Fiacre without guile;
Of Sedulius, hymn-maker when hymns were rare;
Of Scotus the subtle, who clove a hair
Into sixty parts, and had marge to spare.
To her brother I spake of Oisin and Fionn,
And they wept at the death of great Oisin's son.
I taught the heart of the boy to revel
    In tales of old greatness that never tire;
And the virgin's, up-springing from earth's low level,
    To wed with heaven like the altar fire.
I taught her all that a woman should know,
    And that none should teach her worse lore, I gave her
A dagger keen, and taught her the blow
That subdues the knave to discreet behaviour.
A sand-stone there on my knee she set,
And sharpened its point—I can see her yet—
I held back her hair and she sharpen'd the edge,
While the wind piped low through the reeds and
        sedge.

She died in the convent on Ina's height:—
    I saw her the day that she took the veil:
As slender she stood as the Paschal light,
    As tall and slender and bright and pale!
I saw her: and dropped as dead: bereaven
Is earth when her holy ones leave her for heaven.

Her brother fell in the fight at Begh,
May they plead for me both on my dying day!

All praise to the man who brought us the Faith!
'Tis a staff by day and our pillow in death!
All praise I say to that blessed youth,
Who heard in a dream from Tyrawley's strand
That wail, 'Put forth o'er the sea thy hand:
In the dark we die: give us hope and Truth!'
But Patrick built not on Iorras' shore
That convent where now the Franciscans dwell:
Columba was mighty in prayer and war:
But the young monk preaches as loud as his bell,
That love must rule all, and all wrongs be forgiven,
Or else he is sure we shall reach not heaven!
This doctrine I count right cruel and hard,
And when I am laid in the old churchyard,
The habit of Francis I will not wear:
Nor wear I his cord or his cloth of hair
In secret. Men dwindle: till psalm and prayer
Had softened the land no Dane dwelt there!

I forgive old Cathbar who sank my boat:
    Must I pardon Feargal who slew my son:
Or the pirate, Strongbow, who burned Granote,
    They tell me, and in it nine priests, a nun,
And worse—St. Finian's old crozier staff?
At forgiveness like that, I spit and laugh!
My chief in his wine-cups forgave twelve men:
And of these a dozen rebelled again.
There never was chief more brave than he!
    The night he was born Loch Gar up-burst:
He was bard-loving, gift-making, fond of glee,
    The last to fly, to advance the first.

He was like the top spray upon Uladh's oak,
   He was like the tap-root of Argial's pine:
He was secret and sudden: as lightning his stroke:
   There was none that could fathom his hid design.
He slept not: if any man scorned his alliance
He struck the first blow for a frank defiance,
With that look in his face, half night, half light,
Like the lake just blackened yet ridged with white!
There were comely wonders before he died:
The eagle barked, and the Banshee cried,
The witch-elm wept with a blighted bud,
The spray of the torrent was red with blood:
The chief returned from the mountains bound,
Forgot to ask after Bran his hound.
We knew he would die: three days were o'er,
He died. We *waked* him for three days more:
One by one, upon brow and breast,
The whole clan kissed him: In peace may he rest!

I sang his dirge, I could sing that time
Four thousand staves of ancestral rhyme:
To-day I can scarcely sing the half:
Of old I was corn, and I now am chaff!
My song to-day is a breeze that shakes
   Feebly the down on the cygnet's breast;
'Twas then a billow the beach that rakes,
   Or a storm that buffets the mountain's crest.
Whatever I bit with a venomed song,
   Grew sick, were it beast, or tree, or man:
The wronged one sued me to right his wrong
   With the flail of the Satire and fierce Ode's fan.
I sang to the chieftains: each stock I traced,
Lest lines should grow tangled through fraud or haste.
To princes I sang in a loftier tone

Of Moran the just who refused a throne;
Of Moran, whose torque would close, and choke
The wry-necked witness that falsely spoke.
I taught them how to win love and hate,
Not love from all; and to shun debate.
To maids in the bower I sang of love:
And of war at the feastings in bawn or grove.

Great is our Order: but greater far
   Were its pomp and power in the days of old,
When the five Chief Bards in peace or war
   Had thirty bards each in his train enrolled:
When Ollave Fodla in Tara's hall
   Fed bards and kings; when the boy King Nial
Was trained by Torna; when Britain and Gaul
   Sent crowns of laurel to Dallan Forgial.
To-day we can launch the clans into fight;
   That day we could freeze them in mid career!
Whatever man knows was our realm by right:
   The lore without music no Gael would hear.
Old Cormac the brave blind king was bard
Ere fame rose yet of O'Daly and Ward.
The son of Milesius was bard—'Go back
   'My People,' he sang, 'ye have done a wrong!
Nine waves go back o'er the green sea track,
   Let your foes their castles and coasts make strong.
To the island you came by stealth and at night:
She is ours if we win her, in all men's sight;'
For that first song's sake let our bards hold fast
To Truth and Justice from first to last!
'Tis over! some think we erred through pride,
Though Columba the vengeance turned aside.
Too strong we were not: too rich we were:
Give wealth to knaves: 'tis the true man's snare.

But now men lie: they are just no more;
    They forsake the old ways; they quest for new;
They pry and they snuff after strange false lore,
    As dogs hunt vermin: it never was true:—
I have scorned it for twenty years—this babble,
That eastward and southward, a Saxon rabble
Have won great battles and rule large lands,
And plight with daughters of ours their hands.
We know the bold Norman o'erset their throne
Long since. Our lands! let them guard their own.

How long He leaves me—the great God—here!
    Have I sinned some sin, or has God forgotten?
This year, I think, is my hundredth year;
    I am like a bad apple unripe and rotten!
They shall lift me ere long, they shall lay me—the clan,—
By the strength of men on Mount Cruachan!
God has much to think of! How much He hath seen,
And how much is gone by that once hath been!
On sandy hills where the rabbits burrow,
    Are Raths of Kings' men, named not now;
On mountain-tops I have tracked the furrow,
    And found in forests the buried plough.
For one now living the strong land then
Gave kindly food and raiment to ten.
No doubt they waxed proud and their God defied:
    So their harvest He blighted and burned their hoard;
    Or He sent them plagues, or He sent the sword,
Or He sent them lightning and so they died,
Like Dathi the King on the dark Alp's side.
Ah me! that man who is made of dust,
    Should have pride towards God! 'Tis a demon's spleen!
I have often feared lest God the All-just,
    Should bend from heaven and sweep earth clean:

Should sweep us all into corners and holes,
Like dust of the house-floor both bodies and souls!
I have often feared He would send some wind
In wrath; and the nation wake up stone blind.
    In age or in youth we have all wrought ill:
    I say not our great King Nial did well,
Although he was Lord of the Pledges Nine,
    Where besides subduing this land of Eire,
He raised in Armorica banner and sign,
    And wasted the British coast with fire.
Perhaps in His mercy the Lord will say,
'These men, God's help, 'twas a rough boy-play!'
He is certain, that young Franciscan Priest—
God sees great sin where men see least;
Yet this were to give unto God the eye—
Unmeet the thought, of the humming fly!
I trust there are small things He scorns to see
In the lowly who cry to Him piteously.
Our hope is Christ: I have wept full oft,
    He came not to Eire in Oisin's time;
Though love and those new monks would make men soft,
    If they were not hardened by war and rhyme.
I have done my part: my end draws nigh:
I shall leave old Eire with a smile and sigh,
She will miss me not as I missed my son,
Yet for her and her praise were my best deeds done.
Man's deeds! Man's deeds! they are shades that fleet,
Or ripples like those that break at my feet.
The deeds of my chief and the deeds of my king
Grow hazy, far seen, in the hills in spring.
Nothing is great save the death on the cross!
    But Pilate and Herod I hate, and know
    Had Fionn lived then he had laid them low,
Though the world thereby had sustained great loss.

My blindness and deafness and aching back
With meekness I bear for that suffering's sake;
And the Lent-fast for Mary's sake I love,
And the honour of Him, the Man Above!
My songs are all over now:——so best!
They are laid in the heavenly Singer's breast,
Who never sings but a star is born:
May we hear His song in the endless morn!
I give glory to God for our battles won
     By wood or river, on bay or creek:
For Norna——who died; for my father, Conn:
     For feasts, and the chase on the mountains bleak:
I bewail my sins, both unknown and known,
     And of those I have injured forgiveness seek.
The men that were wicked to me and mine
(Not quenching a wrong, nor in war nor wine),
I forgive and absolve them all, save three:
May Christ in His mercy be kind to me!

Aubrey de Vere

LAMENT FOR THE DEATH OF EOGHAN RUADH O'NEILL

'Did they dare, did they dare, to slay Eoghan Ruadh O'Neill?'
'Yes, they slew with poison him they feared to meet with steel.'
'May God wither up their hearts! May their blood cease to flow!
'May they walk in living death, who poisoned Eoghan Ruadh!

'Though it break my heart to hear, say again the bitter words.'
'From Derry, against Cromwell, he marched to measure swords:
But the weapon of the Sassanach met him on his way,
And he died at Cloch Uachtar, upon St. Leonard's day.

'Wail, wail ye for the Mighty One! Wail, wail ye for the Dead!
Quench the hearth, and hold the breath—with ashes strew the head.
How tenderly we loved him! How deeply we deplore!
Holy Saviour! but to think we shall never see him more!

'Sagest in the council was he, kindest in the hall,
Sure we never won a battle—'twas Owen won them all.
Had he lived—had he lived—our dear country had been free;
But he's dead, but he's dead, and 'tis slaves we'll ever be.

'O'Farrell and Clanricarde, Preston and Red Hugh,
Audley and MacMahon—ye are valiant, wise, and true;
But—what are ye all to our darling who is gone?
The Rudder of our Ship was he, our Castle's corner stone!

'Wail, wail him through the Island! Weep, weep for our pride!
Would that on the battle-field our gallant chief had died!
Weep the Victor of Beinn Burb—weep him, young and old;
Weep for him, ye women—your Beautiful lies cold!

'We thought you would not die—we were sure you would not go,
And leave us in our utmost need to Cromwell's cruel blow—
Sheep without a shepherd, when the snow shuts out the sky—
O! why did you leave us, Eoghan? Why did you die?

'Soft as woman's was your voice, O'Neill! bright was your eye,
O! why did you leave us, Eoghan? Why did you die?
Your troubles are all over, you're at rest with God on high,
But we're slaves, and we're orphans, Eoghan!—why did you die?'

Thomas Davis

MAIRE BHAN ASTÓR

In a valley far away,
    With my *Maire bhan astór*,
Short would be the summer-day,
    Ever loving more and more;

Winter days would all grow long,
  With the light her heart would pour,
With her kisses and her song,
  And her loving mait go leór.
    Fond is Maire bhan astór,
    Fair is Maire bhan astór,
    Sweet as ripple on the shore,
    Sings my Maire bhan astór.

O! her sire is very proud,
  And her mother cold as stone;
But her brother bravely vowed
  She should be my bride alone;
For he knew I loved her well,
  And he knew she loved me too,
So he sought their pride to quell,
  But 'twas all in vain to sue.
    True is Maire bhan astór,
    Tried is Maire bhan astór,
    Had I wings I'd never soar
    From my Maire bhan astór.

There are lands where manly toil
  Surely reaps the crop it sows,
Glorious woods and teeming soil,
  Where the broad Missouri flows:
Through the trees the smoke shall rise,
  From our hearth with mait go leór,
There shall shine the happy eyes
  Of my Maire bhan astór.
    Mild is Maire bhan astór,
    Mine is Maire bhan astór,
    Saints will watch about the door
    Of my Maire bhan astór.

                              Thomas Davis

O! THE MARRIAGE
Air—The Swaggering Jig

O! the marriage, the marriage,
    With love and *mo bhuachaill* for me,
The ladies that ride in a carriage
    Might envy my marriage to me;
For Eoghan is straight as a tower,
    And tender and loving and true,
He told me more love in an hour
    Than the Squires of the county could do.
            Then, O! the marriage, etc.

His hair is a shower of soft gold,
    His eye is as clear as the day,
His conscience and vote were unsold
    When others were carried away;
His word is as good as an oath,
    And freely 'twas given to me;
O! sure 'twill be happy for both
    The day of our marriage to see.
            Then, O! the marriage, etc.

His kinsmen are honest and kind,
    The neighbours think much of his skill,
And Eoghan's the lad to my mind,
    Though he owns neither castle nor mill.
But he has a tilloch of land,
    A horse, and a stocking of coin,
A foot for a dance, and a hand
    In the cause of his country to join.
            Then, O! the marriage, etc.

We meet in the market and fair—
    We meet in the morning and night—

He sits on the half of my chair,
   And my people are wild with delight.
Yet I long through the winter to skim,
   Though Eoghan longs more, I can see,
When I will be married to him,
   And he will be married to me.
Then, O! the marriage, the marriage,
   With love and *mo bhuachaill* for me,
The ladies that ride in a carriage
   Might envy my marriage to me.

                                        Thomas Davis

A PLEA FOR LOVE

The summer brook flows in the bed,
   The winter torrent tore asunder;
The skylark's gentle wings are spread
   Where walk the lightning and the thunder;
And thus you'll find the sternest soul
   The gayest tenderness concealing,
And minds that seem to mock control,
   Are ordered by some fairy feeling.

Then, maiden! start not from the hand
   That's hardened by the swaying sabre—
The pulse beneath may be as bland
   As evening after day of labour:
And, maiden! start not from the brow
   That thought has knit, and passion darkened—
In twilight hours, 'neath forest bough,
   The tenderest tales are often hearkened.

                                        Thomas Davis

REMEMBRANCE

Cold in the earth—and the deep snow piled above thee,
    Far, far removed, cold in the dreary grave!
Have I forgot, my only Love, to love thee,
    Severed at last by Time's all-severing wave?

Now, when alone, do my thoughts no longer hover
    Over the mountains, on that northern shore,
Resting their wings where heath and fern-leaves cover
    Thy noble heart for ever, ever more?

Cold in the earth—and fifteen wild Decembers,
    From these brown hills, have melted into spring!
Faithful, indeed, is the spirit that remembers
    After such years of change and suffering!

Sweet Love of youth, forgive, if I forget thee,
    While the world's tide is bearing me along;
Other desires and other hopes beset me,
    Hopes which obscure, but cannot do thee wrong;

No later light has lighted up my heaven,
    No second morn has ever shone for me;
All my life's bliss from thy dear life was given,
    All my life's bliss is in the grave with thee.

But, when the days of golden dreams had perished,
    And even Despair was powerless to destroy;
Then did I learn how existence could be cherished,
    Strengthened and fed without the aid of joy.

Then did I check the tears of useless passion—
    Weaned my young soul from yearning after thine;
Sternly denied its burning wish to hasten,
    Down to that tomb already more than mine.

And, even yet, I dare not let it languish,
    Dare not indulge in memory's rapturous pain;
Once drinking deep of that divinest anguish
    How could I seek the empty world again?

Emily Brontë

A FRAGMENT FROM 'THE PRISONER: A FRAGMENT'

Still, let my tyrants know, I am not doomed to wear
Year after year in gloom, and desolate despair;
A messenger of Hope comes every night to me,
And offers for short life, eternal liberty.

He comes with Western winds, with evening's wandering airs,
With that clear dusk of heaven that brings the thickest stars.
Winds take a pensive tone, and stars a tender fire,
And visions rise, and change, that kill me with desire.

Desire for nothing known in my maturer years,
When Joy grew mad with awe, at counting future tears.
When, if my spirit's sky was full of flashes warm,
I knew not whence they came, from sun or thunder-storm.

But first, a hush of peace—a soundless calm descends;
The struggle of distress, and fierce impatience ends.
Mute music soothes my breast—unuttered harmony
That I could never dream, till Earth was lost to me.

Then dawns the Invisible; the Unseen its truth reveals;
My outward sense is gone, my inward essence feels:
Its wings are almost free—its home, its harbour found,
Measuring the gulf, it stoops, and dares the final bound.

O, dreadful is the check—intense the agony—
When the ear begins to hear, and the eye begins to see;
When the pulse begins to throb,—the brain to think again,
The soul to feel the flesh, and the flesh to feel the chain.

Yet I would lose no sting, would wish no torture less,
The more that anguish racks, the earlier it will bless;
And robed in fires of hell, or bright with heavenly shine,
If it but herald death, the vision is divine.

                                                    Emily Brontë

LAST LINES

No coward soul is mine,
No trembler in the world's storm-troubled sphere:
    I see Heaven's glories shine,
And faith shines equal, arming me from fear.

O God, within my breast,
Almighty, ever-present Deity!
    Life—that in me has rest,
As I—undying Life—have power in Thee.

Vain are the thousand creeds
That move men's hearts: unutterably vain;
    Worthless as withered weeds,
Or idlest froth amid the boundless main,

To waken doubt in one
Holding so fast to Thine infinity;
    So surely anchored on
The steadfast rock of immortality,

With wide-embracing love
Thy spirit animates eternal years,
    Pervades and broods above,
Changes, sustains, dissolves, creates, and rears.

Though earth and man were gone,
And suns and universes ceased to be,
    And Thou were left alone,
Every existence would exist in Thee.

There is not room for Death,
Nor atom that his might could render void:
Thou—Thou art Being and Breath,
And what Thou art may never be destroyed.

Emily Brontë

THE MEMORY OF THE DEAD

Who fears to speak of Ninety-eight?
  Who blushes at the name?
When cowards mock the patriot's fate,
  Who hange his head for shame?
He's all a knave or half a slave
  Who slights his country thus;
But a true man, like you, man,
  Will fill your glass with us.

We drink the memory of the brave,
  The faithful and the few—
Some lie far off beyond the wave,
  Some sleep in Ireland, too;
All, all are gone—but still lives on
  The fame of those who died;
All true men, like you, men,
  Remember them with pride.

Some on the shores of distant lands
  Their weary hearts have laid,
And by the stranger's heedless hands
  Their lonely graves were made;
But, though their clay be far away
  Beyond the Atlantic foam,
In true men, like you, men,
  Their spirit's still at home.

The dust of some is Irish earth;
    Among their own they rest;
And the same land that gave them birth
    Has caught them to her breast;
And we will pray that from their clay
    Full many a race may start
Of true men, like you, men,
    To act as brave a part.

They rose in dark and evil days
    To right their native land;
They kindled here a living blaze
    That nothing shall withstand.
Alas! that Might can vanquish Right—
    They fell, and passed away;
But true men, like you, men,
    Are plenty here to-day.

Then here's their memory—may it be
    For us a guiding light,
To cheer our strife for liberty,
    And teach us to unite!
Through good and ill, be Ireland's still,
    Though sad as theirs your fate;
And true men, be you, men,
    Like those of Ninety-Eight.

John Kells Ingram

THE WINDING BANKS OF ERNE; OR, THE EMIGRANT'S ADIEU TO BALLYSHANNY

Adieu to Ballyshanny! where I was bred and born;
Go where I may, I'll think of you, as sure as night and morn;
The kindly spot, the friendly town, where every one is known,
And not a face in all the place but partly seems my own;
There's not a house or window, there's not a field or hill,
But East or West, in foreign lands, I'll recollect them still.
I leave my warm heart with you, tho' my back I'm forced to
    turn—
So adieu to Ballyshanny, and the winding banks of Erne!

No more on pleasant evenings we'll saunter down the Mall,
When the trout is rising to the fly, the salmon to the fall.
The boat comes straining on her net, and heavily she creeps,
Cast off, cast off—she feels the oars, and to her berth she sweeps;
Now fore and aft keep hauling, and gathering up the clew,
Till a silver wave of salmon rolls in among the crew.
Then they may sit, with pipes a-lit, and many a joke and
    'yarn':—
Adieu to Ballyshanny, and the winding banks of Erne!

The music of the waterfall, the mirror of the tide,
When all the green-hill'd harbour is full from side to side,
From Portnasun to Bulliebawns, and round the Abbey Bay,
From rocky Inis Saimer to Coolnargit sandhills gray;
While far upon the southern line, to guard it like a wall,
The Leitrim mountains clothed in blue gaze calmly over all,
And watch the ship sail up or down, the red flag at her stern;—
Adieu to these, adieu to all the winding banks of Erne!

Farewell to you, Kildoney lads, and them that pull an oar,
A lug-sail set, or haul a net, from the Point to Mullaghmore;
From Killybegs to bold Slieve-League, that ocean-mountain
    steep,

Six hundred yards in air aloft, six hundred in the deep;
From Dooran to the Fairy Bridge, and round by Tullen strand,
Level and long, and white with waves, where gull and curlew
    stand;
Head out to sea when on your lee the breakers you discern!—
Adieu to all the billowy coast, and winding banks of Erne!

Farewell, Coolmore,—Bundoran! and your summer crowds that
    run
From inland homes to see with joy th' Atlantic setting sun;
To breathe the buoyant salted air, and sport among the waves;
To gather shells on sandy beach, and tempt the gloomy caves;
To watch the flowing, ebbing tide, the boats, the crabs, the fish;
Young men and maids to meet and smile, and form a tender
    wish;
The sick and old in search of health, for all things have their turn—
And I must quit my native shore, and the winding banks of Erne!

Farewell to every white cascade from the Harbour to Belleek,
And every pool where fins may rest, and ivy-shaded creek;
The sloping fields, the lofty rocks, where ash and holly grow,
The one split yew-tree gazing on the curving flood below;
The Lough that winds through islands under Turaw mountain
    green;
And Castle Caldwell's stretching woods, with tranquil bays
    between;
And Breesie Hill, and many a pond among the heath and fern;—
For I must say adieu—adieu to the winding banks of Erne!

The thrush will call through Camlin groves the live-long summer
    day;
The waters run by mossy cliff, and banks with wild flowers gay;
The girls will bring their work and sing beneath a twisted
    thorn,
Or stray with sweethearts down the path among the growing corn;

Along the river-side they go, where I have often been,—
O never shall I see again the days that I have seen!
A thousand chances are to one I never may return,—
Adieu to Ballyshanny, and the winding banks of Erne!

Adieu to evening dances, when merry neighbours meet,
And the fiddle says to boys and girls, 'Get up and shake your feet!'
To *shanachus* and wise old talk of Erin's days gone by—
Who trench'd the rath on such a hill, and where the bones may
    lie
Of saint, or king, or warrior chief; with tales of fairy power,
And tender ditties sweetly sung to pass the twilight hour.
The mournful song of exile is now for me to learn—
Adieu, my dear companions on the winding banks of Erne!

Now measure from the Commons down to each end of the Purt,
Round the Abbey, Moy, and Knather,—I wish no one any hurt;
The Main Street, Back Street, College Lane, the Mall, and
    Portnasun,
If any foes of mine are there, I pardon every one.
I hope that man and womankind will do the same by me;
For my heart is sore and heavy at voyaging the sea.
My loving friends I'll bear in mind, and often fondly turn
To think of Ballyshanny and the winding banks of Erne!

If ever I'm a money'd man, I mean, please God, to cast
My golden anchor in the place where youthful years were past;
Though heads that now are black and brown must meanwhile
    gather gray,
New faces rise by every hearth, and old ones drop away—
Yet dearer still that Irish hill than all the world beside;
It's home, sweet home, where'er I roam, through lands and
    waters wide.
And if the Lord allows me, I surely will return
To my native Ballyshanny, and the winding banks of Erne.

                                        William Allingham

THE FAIRIES

Up the airy mountain,
    Down the rushy glen,
We daren't go a-hunting
    For fear of little men;
Wee folk, good folk,
    Trooping all together;
Green jacket, red cap,
    And white owl's feather!

Down along the rocky shore
    Some make their home,
They live on crispy pancakes,
    Of yellow tide-foam;
Some in the reeds
    Of the bleak mountain lake,
With frogs for their watch-dogs,
    All night awake.

High on the hill-top
    The old King sits;
He is now so old and gray
    He's nigh lost his wits.
With a bridge of white mist
    Columbkill he crosses,
On his stately journeys
    From Sleeveleague to Rosses;
Or going up with music
    On cold starry nights,
To sup with the Queen
    Of the gay Northern Lights.

They stole little Bridget
    For seven years long;

When she came down again
   Her friends were all gone.
They took her lightly back,
   Between the night and morrow,
They thought that she was fast asleep,
   But she was dead with sorrow.
They have kept her ever since
   Deep within the lake,
On a bed of flag-leaves,
   Watching till she wake.

By the craggy hillside
   Through the mosses bare,
They have planted thorn-trees
   For pleasure here and there.
If any man so daring
   As dig them up in spite,
He shall find their sharpest thorns
   In his bed at night.

Up the airy mountain,
   Down the rushy glen,
We daren't go a-hunting
   For fear of little men;
Wee folk, good folk,
   Trooping all together;
Green jacket, red cap,
   And white owl's feather!

William Allingham

THE ABBOT OF INISFALEN
A Killarney legend

The Abbot of Inisfālen awoke ere dawn of day;
Under the dewy green leaves went he forth to pray.
The lake around his island lay smooth and dark and deep,
And wrapped in a misty stillness the mountains were all asleep.
Low kneel'd the Abbot Cormac when the dawn was dim and
    gray,
The prayers of his holy office he faithfully 'gan say.
Low kneel'd the Abbot Cormac while the dawn was waxing red;
And for his sins' forgiveness a solemn prayer he said:
Low kneel'd that holy Abbot while the dawn was waking clear,
And he prayed with loving-kindness for his convent-brethren
    dear.
Low kneel'd the blessed Abbot while the dawn was waxing
    bright;
He pray'd a great prayer for Ireland, he pray'd with all his might.
Low kneel'd that good old Father while the sun began to dart;
He pray'd a prayer for all men, he pray'd it from his heart.
His blissful soul was in Heaven, tho' a breathing man was he;
He was out of time's dominion, so far as the living may be.

The Abbot of Inisfālen arose upon his feet;
He heard a small bird singing, and O but it sung sweet!
It sung upon a holly-bush, this little snow-white bird;
A song so full of gladness he never before had heard,
It sung upon a hazel, it sung upon a thorn;
He had never heard such music since the hour that he was
    born.
It sung upon a sycamore, it sung upon a briar;
To follow the song and hearken the Abbot would never tire.
Till at last he well bethought him, he might no longer stay;
So he bless'd the little white singing-bird, and gladly went his
    way.

But, when he came to his Abbey, he found a wondrous
   wondrous change;
He saw no friendly faces there, for every face was strange.
The strange men spoke unto him; and he heard from all and
   each
The foreign tongue of the Sassenach, not wholesome Irish
   speech.
Then the oldest monk came forward, in Irish tongue spake he:
'Thou wearest the holy Augustine's dress, and who hath given it
   to thee?'
'I wear the holy Augustine's dress, and Cormac is my name,
The Abbot of this good Abbey by grace of God I am.

I went forth to pray, at the dawn of day; and when my prayers
   were said,
I hearken'd awhile to a little bird, that sang above my head.'
The monks to him made answer, 'Two hundred years have gone
   o'er,
Since our Abbot Cormac went through the gate, and never was
   heard of more.
Matthias now is our Abbot, and twenty have pass'd away.
The stranger is lord of Ireland; we live in an evil day.
Days will come and go,' he said, 'and the world will pass away:
In Heaven a day is a thousand years, a thousand years are a day.'

'Now give me absolution; for my time is come,' said he.
And they gave him absolution, as speedily as might be.
Then, close outside the window, the sweetest song they heard
That ever yet since the world began was utter'd by any bird.
The monks look'd out and saw the bird, its feathers all white and
   clean;
And then in a moment, beside it, another white bird was seen.
Those two they sang together, waved their white wings, and
   fled;
Flew aloft and vanish'd; but the good old man was dead.

They buried his blessed body where lake and green-sward meet,
A carven cross above his head, a holly-bush at his feet;
Where spreads the beautiful water to gay or cloudy skies,
And the purple peaks of Killarney from ancient woods arise.

William Allingham

TWILIGHT VOICES

Now, at the hour when ignorant mortals
    Drowse in the shade of their whirling sphere,
Heaven and Hell from invisible portals
    Breathing comfort and ghastly fear,
        Voices I hear;
I hear strange voices, flitting, calling,
    Wavering by on the dusky blast,—
'Come, let us go, for the night is falling;
    Come, let us go, for the day is past!'

Troops of joys are they, now departed?
    Winged hopes that no longer stay?
Guardian spirits grown weary-hearted?
    Powers that have linger'd their latest day?
        What do they say?
What do they sing? I hear them calling,
    Whispering, gathering, flying fast,—
'Come, come, for the night is falling;
    Come, come, for the day is past!'

Sing they to me?—'Thy taper's wasted;
    Mortal, thy sands of life run low;
Thine hours like a flock of birds have hasted:
    Time is ending;—we go, we go.'
        Sing they so?
Mystical voices, floating, calling;
    Dim farewells—the last, the last?

'Come, come away, the night is falling;
   Come, come away, the day is past.'

See, I am ready, Twilight voices!
   Child of the spirit-world am I;
How should I fear you? my soul rejoices,
   O speak plainer! O draw nigh!
      Fain would I fly!
Tell me your message, Ye who are calling
   Out of the dimness vague and vast;
Lift me, take me,—the night is falling;
   Quick, let us go,—the day is past.

William Allingham

FOUR DUCKS ON A POND

Four ducks on a pond,
A grass-bank beyond,
A blue sky of spring,
White clouds on the wing:
What a little thing
To remember for years—
To remember with tears!

William Allingham

THE LOVER AND BIRDS

Within a budding grove,
In April's ear sang every bird his best,
But not a song to pleasure my unrest,
   Or touch the tears unwept of bitter love;
Some spake, methought, with pity, some as if in jest.

To every word
Of every bird
I listen'd, or replied as it behove.

Scream'd Chaffinch, 'Sweet, sweet, sweet!
Pretty lovely, come and meet me here!'
'Chaffinch,' quoth I, 'be dumb awhile, in fear
Thy darling prove no better than a cheat,
And never come, or fly when wintry days appear.'
Yet from a twig,
With voice so big,
The little fowl his utterance did repeat.

Then I, 'The man forlorn
Hears Earth send up a foolish noise aloft.'
'And what 'll he do? What 'll he do?' scoff'd
The Blackbird, standing, in ancient thorn,
Then spread his sooty wings and flitted to the croft
With cackling laugh;
Whom I, being half
Enraged, called after, giving back his scorn.

Worse mock'd the Thrush, 'Die! die!
O, could he do it? could he do it? Nay!
Be quick! be quick! Here, here, here!' (went his lay).
'Take heed! take heed!' then, 'Why? why? why? why? why?
See-ee now! see-ee now!' (he drawl'd) 'Back! back! back!
R-r-r-run away!'
O Thrush, be still!
Or at thy will
Seek some less sad interpreter than I.

'Air, air! blue air and white!
Whither I flee, whither, O whither, O whither I flee!'
(Thus the Lark hurried, mounting from the lea)
'Hills, countries, many waters glittering bright

Whither I see, whither I see! deeper, deeper, deeper, whither
    I see, see, see!'
             'Gay Lark,' I said,
             'The song that's bred
In happy nest may well to heaven make flight.'

'There's something, something sad
I half remember'—piped a broken strain.
Well sung, sweet Robin! Robin sung again.
    'Spring's opening cheerily, cheerily! be we glad!'
Which moved, I wist not why, me melancholy mad,
            Till now, grown meek,
            With wetted cheek,
Most comforting and gentle thoughts I had.

                    William Allingham

THE CELTS

Long, long ago, beyond the misty space
    Of twice a thousand years,
In Erin old there dwelt a mighty race
    Taller than Roman spears;
Like oaks and towers, they had a giant grace,
    Were fleet as deers:
With winds and waves they made their biding-place,
    The Western shepherd seers.

Their ocean-god was *Mananan Mac Lir*,
    Whose angry lips
In their white foam full often would inter
    Whole fleets of ships:
Crom was their day-god, and their thunderer
    Made morning and eclipse:
Bride was their queen of song, and unto her
    They pray'd with fire-touch'd lips.

Great were their acts, their passions, and their sports;
  With clay and stone
They piled on strath and shore those mystic forts,
  Not yet undone;
On cairn-crown'd hills they held their council courts;
  While youths—alone—
With giant-dogs, explored the elks' resorts,
  And brought them down.

Of these was Finn, the father of the bard
  Whose ancient song
Over the clamour of all change is heard,
  Sweet-voiced and strong.
Finn once o'ertook Granu, the golden-hair'd,
  The fleet and young:
From her, the lovely, and from him, the feared,
  The primal poet sprung—

Ossian!—two thousand years of mist and change
  Surround thy name;
Thy Finnian heroes now no longer range
  The hills of Fame.
The very name of Finn and Gael sound strange;
  Yet thine the same
By miscall'd lake and desecrated grange
  Remains, and shall remain!

The Druid's altar and the Druid's creed
  We scarce can trace;
There is not left an undisputed deed
  Of all your race—
Save your majestic Song, which hath their speed,
  And strength, and grace:
In that sole song they live, and love, and bleed—
  It bears them on through space.

Inspirèd giant, shall we e'er behold,
    In our own time,
One fit to speak your spirit on the wold,
    Or seize your rhyme?
One pupil of the past, as mighty-soul'd
    As in the prime
Were the fond, fair, and beautiful, and bold—
    They of your song sublime?

                Thomas D'Arcy McGee

SALUTATION TO THE CELTS

Hail to our Celtic brethren wherever they may be,
In the far woods of Oregon, or o'er the Atlantic sea;
Whether they guard the banner of St. George, in Indian vales,
Or spread beneath the nightless North experimental sails—
          One in name, and in fame,
            Are the sea-divided Gaels.

Though fallen the state of Erin, and changed the Scottish land,
Though small the power of Mona, though unwaked Llewellyn's
    band,
Though Ambrose Merlin's prophecies are held as idle tales,
Though Iona's ruined cloisters are swept by northern gales:
          One in name, and in fame,
            Are the sea-divided Gaels.

In Northern Spain and Italy our brethren also dwell,
And brave are the traditions of their fathers that they tell:
The Eagle or the Crescent in the dawn of history pales
Before the advancing banners of the great Rome-conquering
    Gales.
          One in name, and in fame,
            Are the sea-divided Gaels.

A greeting and a promise unto them all we send;
Their character our charter is, their glory is our end—
Their friend shall be our friend, our foe whoe'er assails
The glory or the story of the sea-divided Gaels.
        One in name, and in fame,
          Are the sea-divided Gaels.

                  Thomas D'Arcy McGee

THE GOBBAN SAOR

He stepped a man, out on the ways of men,
   And no one knew his sept, or rank, or name;
Like a strong stream far issuing from a glen,
   From some source unexplored the Master came;
Gossips there were who, wondrous keen of ken,
   Surmised that he must be a child of shame;
Others declared him of the Druids, then—
   Thro' Patrick's labours—fallen from power and fame.

He lived apart, wrapt up in many plans;
   He wooed not women, tasted not of wine;
He shunned the sports and councils of the clans;
   Nor ever knelt at a frequented shrine.
His orisons were old poetic ranns
   Which the new Olamhs deem'd an evil sign;
To most he seemed one of those Pagan Khans
   Whose mystic vigour knows no cold decline.

He was the builder of the wondrous Towers,
   Which, tall and straight and exquisitely round,
Rise monumental round this isle of ours,
   Index-like, marking spots of holy ground.
In glooming silent glens, in lowland bowers,
   On river banks, these *Cloichteachs* old abound,

Where Art, enraptured, meditates long hours
    And Science ponders, wondering and spell-bound.

Lo, wheresoe'er these pillar-towers aspire,
    Heroes and holy men repose below;
The bones of some, gleaned from a Pagan pyre,
    Others in armour lie, as for a foe;
It was the mighty Master's life-desire
    To chronicle his great ancestors so;
What holier duty, what achievement higher
    Remains to us, than this he thus doth show?

Yet he, the builder, died an unknown death;
    His labours done, no man beheld him more;
'Twas thought his body faded like a breath—
    Or, like a sea-mist, floated off Life's shore.
Doubt overhangs his fate—and faith—and birth:
    His works alone attest his life and love,
They are the only witnesses he hath,
    All else Egyptian darkness covers o'er.

Men called him Gobban Saor, and many a tale
    Yet lingers in the byways of the land,
Of how he cleft the rock, and down the vale
    Led the bright river, child-like, in his hand;
Of how on giant ships he spread great sail
    And many marvels else, by him first planned,
And tho' these legends fail, in Innisfail
    His name and Towers for centuries still shall stand.

Thomas D'Arcy McGee

PATRICK SHEEHAN

My name is Patrick Sheehan,
My years are thirty-four,

Tipperary is my native place,
    Not far from Galtymore;
I came of honest parents,
    But now they're lying low;
And many a pleasant day I spent
    In the Glen of Aherlow.

My father died; I closed his eyes
    Outside our cabin-door;
The landlord and the sheriff too
    Were there the day before!
And then my loving mother,
    And sisters three also,
Were forced to go with broken hearts
    From the Glen of Aherlow.

For three long months, in search of work,
    I wandered far and near;
I went then to the poor-house,
    For to see my mother dear;
The news I heard nigh broke my heart;
    But still, in all my woe,
I blessed the friends who made their graves
    In the Glen of Aherlow.

Bereft of home and kith and kin,
    With plenty all around,
I starved within my cabin,
    And slept upon the ground;
But cruel as my lot was,
    I ne'er did hardship know
'Till I joined the English army,
    Far away from Aherlow.

'Rouse up, there,' says the Corporal,
    'You lazy Hirish hound;

Why don't you hear, you sleepy dog,
    The call "to arms" sound?'
Alas, I had been dreaming
    Of days long, long ago;
I woke before Sebastopol,
    And not in Aherlow.

I groped to find my musket—
    How dark I thought the night!
O blessed God, it was not dark,
    It was the broad daylight!
And when I found that I was blind,
    My tears began to flow;
I longed for even a pauper's grave
    In the Glen of Aherlow.

O blessed Virgin Mary,
    Mine is a mournful tale;
A poor blind prisoner here I am,
    In Dublin's dreary gaol;
Struck blind within the trenches,
    Where I never feared the foe;
And now I'll never see again
    My own sweet Aherlow.

A poor neglected mendicant,
    I wandered through the street;
My nine months' pension now being out,
    I beg from all I meet:
As I joined my country's tyrants,
    My face I'll never show
Among the kind old neighbours
    In the Glen of Aherlow.

Then, Irish youths, dear countrymen,
    Take heed of what I say;

For if you join the English ranks,
    You'll surely rue the day;
And whenever you are tempted
    A-soldiering to go,
Remember poor blind Sheehan
    Of the Glen of Aherlow.

Charles J. Kickham

THE IRISH PEASANT GIRL

She lived beside the Anner,
    At the foot of Sliev-na-mon,
A gentle peasant girl,
    With mild eyes like the dawn;
Her lips were dewy rosebuds;
    Her teeth of pearls rare;
And a snow-drift 'neath a beechen bough
    Her neck and nut-brown hair.

How pleasant 'twas to meet her
    On Sunday, when the bell
Was filling with its mellow tones
    Lone wood and grassy dell!
And when at eve young maidens
    Strayed the river-bank along,
The widow's brown-haired daughter
    Was loveliest of the throng.

O brave, brave Irish girls—
    We well may call you brave!—
Sure the least of all your perils
    Is the stormy ocean wave,
When you leave our quiet valleys,
    And cross the Atlantic's foam,

To hoard your hard-won earnings
    For the helpless ones at home.

'Write word to my own dear mother—
    Say, we'll meet with God above;
And tell my little brothers
    I send them all my love;
May the angels ever guard them,
    Is their dying sister's prayer'—
And folded in the letter
    Was a braid of nut-brown hair.

Ah, cold, and well-nigh callous,
    This weary heart has grown
For thy helpless fate, dear Ireland,
    And for sorrows of my own;
Yet a tear my eye will moisten
    When by Anner's side I stray,
For the lily of the mountain foot
    That withered far away.

                    Charles J. Kickham

TO GOD AND IRELAND TRUE

I sit beside my darling's grave,
    Who in the prison died,
And tho' my tears fall thick and fast,
    I think of him with pride:—
Ay, softly fall my tears like dew,
For one to God and Ireland true.

'I love my God o'er all,' he said,
    'And then I love my land,
And next I love my Lily sweet,
    Who pledged me her white hand:—

To each—to all—I'm ever true,
To God—to Ireland and to you.'

No tender nurse his hard bed smoothed
    Or softly raised his head:—
He fell asleep and woke in heaven
    Ere I knew he was dead;—
Yet why should I my darling rue?
He was to God and Ireland true.

O, 'tis a glorious memory;
    I'm prouder than a queen
To sit beside my hero's grave
    And think on what has been:—
And O, my darling, I am true
To God—to Ireland and to you!

Ellen O'Leary

THE BANSHEE

Green, in the wizard arms,
Of the foam-bearded Atlantic,
An isle of old enchantment,
A melancholy isle,
Enchanted and dreaming lies;
And there, by Shannon's flowing,
In the moonlight, spectre thin,
The spectre Erin sits.

An aged desolation
She sits by old Shannon's flowing,
A mother of many children,
Of children exiled and dead,
In her home, with bent head, homeless,

Clasping her knees she sits,
Keening, keening!

And at her keene the fairy-grass
Trembles on dun and barrow;
Around the foot of her ancient crosses
The grave-grass shakes and the nettle swings;
In haunted glens the meadow-sweet
Flings to the night-wind
Her mystic mournful perfume;
The sad spearmint by holy wells
Breathes melancholy balm.

Sometimes she lifts her head,
With blue eyes tearless,
And gazes athwart the reek of night
Upon things long past,
Upon things to come.

And sometimes, when the moon
Brings tempest upon the deep,
And roused Atlantic thunders from his caverns in the West,
The wolf-hound at her feet
Springs up with a mighty bay,
And chords of mystery sound from the wild harp at her side,

Strung from the heart of poets;
And she flies on the verge of the tempest
Around her shuddering isle,
With grey hair streaming:
A meteor of evil omen,
The spectre of hope forlorn,
Keening, keening!

She keenes, and the strings of her wild harp shiver
On the gusts of night:
O'er the four waters she keenes—over Moyle she keenes,

O'er the Sea of Milith, and the Strait of Strongbow,
And the Ocean of Columbus.

And the Fianna hear, and the ghosts of her cloudy hovering heroes;
And the swan, Fianoula, wails o'er the waters of Inisfail,
Chanting her song of destiny,
The rune of the weaving Fates.

And the nations hear in the void and quaking time of night,
Sad unto dawning, dirges,
Solemn dirges,
And snatches of bardic song;
Their souls quake in the void and quaking time of night,
And they dream of the weird of kings,
And tyrannies moulting, sick
In the dreadful wind of change.

Wail no more, lonely one, mother of exiles, wail no more,
Banshee of the world—no more!
Thy sorrows are the world's, thou art no more alone;
Thy wrongs, the world's.

John Todhunter

AGHADOE

There's a glade in Aghadoe, Aghadoe, Aghadoe,
There's a green and silent glade in Aghadoe,
Where we met, my Love and I, Love's fair planet in the sky,
O'er that sweet and silent glade in Aghadoe.

There's a glen in Aghadoe, Aghadoe, Aghadoe,
There's a deep and secret glen in Aghadoe,
Where I hid from the eyes of the red-coats and their spies
That year the trouble came to Aghadoe.

O! my curse on one black heart in Aghadoe, Aghadoe,
On Shaun Dhuv, my mother's son in Aghadoe,

When your throat fries in hell's drouth salt the flame be in your
    mouth,
For the treachery you did in Aghadoe!

For they tracked me to that glen in Aghadoe, Aghadoe,
When the price was on his head in Aghadoe;
O'er the mountain through the wood, as I stole to him with food,
When in hiding lone he lay in Aghadoe.

But they never took him living in Aghadoe, Aghadoe;
With the bullets in his heart in Aghadoe,
There he lay, the head—my breast keeps the warmth where once
    'twould rest—
Gone, to win the traitor's gold, from Aghadoe!

I walked to Mallow Town from Aghadoe, Aghadoe,
Brought his head from the gaol's gate to Aghadoe,
Then I covered him with fern, and I piled on him the cairn.
Like an Irish King he sleeps in Aghadoe.

O! to creep into that cairn in Aghadoe, Aghadoe!
There to rest upon his breast in Aghadoe!
Sure your dog for you could die with no truer heart than I,
Your own love, cold on your cairn in Aghadoe.

John Todhunter

A MAD SONG

I hear the wind a-blowing,
I hear the corn a-growing,
I hear the Virgin praying,
I hear what she is saying.

Hester Sigerson

LADY MARGARET'S SONG

Girls, when I am gone away,
  On this bosom strew
Only flowers meek and pale,
  And the yew.

Lay these hands down by my side,
  Let my face be bare;
Bind a kerchief round the face,
  Smooth my hair.

Let my bier be borne at dawn,
  Summer grows so sweet,
Deep into the forest green
  Where boughs meet.

Then pass away, and let me lie
  One long, warm, sweet day
There alone, with face upturned,
  One sweet day.

While the morning light grows broad,
  While noon sleepeth sound,
While the evening falls and faints,
  While the world goes round.

Edward Dowden

SONG

I made another garden, yea,
  For my new Love.
I left the dead rose where it lay
  And set the new above.
Why did my Summer not begin?
  Why did my heart not haste?

My old Love came and walked therein
    And laid the garden waste.

She entered with her weary smile,
    Just as of old:
She looked around a little while
    And shivered with the cold.
Her passing touch was death to all,
    Her passing look a blight;
She made the white rose-petals fall,
    And turned the red rose white.

Her pale robe clinging to the grass
    Seemed like a snake
That bit the grass and ground, alas!
    And a sad trail did make.
She went up slowly to the gate,
    And then, just as of yore,
She turned back at the last to wait
    And say farewell once more.

                Arthur O'Shaughnessy

FATHER O'FLYNN

Of priests we can offer a charming variety,
Far renowned for larnin' and piety,
Still I'd advance you, without impropriety,
    Father O'Flynn as the flower of them all.
        Here's a health to you, Father O'Flynn,
        Slainte, and *slainte*, and *slainte* agin.
           Powerfullest preacher,
           And tindherest teacher,
    And kindliest creature in Old Donegal.

Talk of your Provost and Fellows of Trinity,
Far renowned for Greek and Latinity,

Gad! and the divils and all at Divinity,
    Father O'Flynn would make hares of them all.
        Come, I venture to give you my word,
        Never the likes of his logic was heard,
           Down from mythology,
           Into thayology,
    Troth and conchology, if he'd the call.

Father O'Flynn, you've the wonderful way with you,
All the old sinners are wishful to pray with you,
All the young children are wild for to play with you,
    You've such a way with you, Father *avick*!
        Still for all you're so gentle a soul,
        Gad, you've your flock in the grandest control;
           Checking the crazy ones,
           Coaxing unaisy ones,
    Lifting the lazy ones on with the stick.

And though quite avoiding all foolish frivolity,
Still at all seasons of innocent jollity,
Where is the play-boy can claim an equality
    At comicality, Father, with you?
        Once the Bishop looked grave at your jest,
        Till this remark set him off with the rest:
           'Is it leave gaiety
           All to the laity?
Cannot the clargy be Irishmen too?'

                        Alfred Perceval Graves

SONG

The silent bird is hid in the boughs,
    The scythe is hid in the corn,
The lazy oxen wink and drowse,
    The grateful sheep are shorn.

Redder and redder burns the rose,
    The lily was ne'er so pale,
Stiller and stiller the river flows
    Along the path to the vale.

A little door is hid in the boughs,
    A face is hiding within;
When birds are silent and oxen drowse,
    Why should a maiden spin?
Slower and slower turns the wheel,
    The face turns red and pale,
Brighter and brighter the looks that steal,
    Along the path to the vale.

Rosa Gilbert

REQUIESCAT

Tread lightly, she is near
    Under the snow,
Speak gently, she can hear
    The daisies grow.

All her bright golden hair,
    Tarnished with rust,
She that was young and fair
    Fallen to dust.

Lily-like, white as snow,
    She hardly knew
She was a woman, so
    Sweetly she grew.

Coffin-board, heavy stone
    Lie on her breast,
I vex my heart alone,
    She is at rest.

Peace, Peace, she cannot hear
　Lyre or sonnet,
All my life's buried here,
　Heap earth upon it.

Oscar Wilde

THE LAMENT OF QUEEN MAEV
From the Irish of the Book of Leinster

Raise the cromlech high!
　Mac Moghcorb is slain,
And other men's renown
　Has leave to live again.

Cold at last he lies
　'Neath the burial stone.
All the blood he shed
　Could not save his own.

Stately, strong he went,
　Through his nobles all,
When we paced together
　Up the banquet-hall.

Dazzling white as lime,
　Was his body fair,
Cherry-red his cheeks,
　Raven-black his hair.

Razor-sharp his spear,
　And the shield he bore,
High as champion's head—
　His arm was like an oar.

Never aught but truth
　Spake my noble king;

Valour all his trust
 In all his warfaring.

As the forkèd pole
 Holds the roof-tree's weight,
So my hero's arm
 Held the battle straight.

Terror went before him,
 Death behind his back,
Well the wolves of Erinn
 Knew his chariot's track.

Seven bloody battles
 He broke upon his foes,
In each a hundred heroes
 Fell beneath his blows.

Once he fought at Fossud,
 Thrice at Ath-finn-fail.
'Twas my king that conquered
 At bloody Ath-an-Scail.

At the Boundary Stream
 Fought the Royal Hound,
And for Bernas battle
 Stands his name renowned.

Here he fought with Leinster—
 Last of all his frays—
On the Hill of Cucorb's Fate
 High his cromlech raise.

T. W. Rolleston

THE DEAD AT CLONMACNOIS
From the Irish of Enoch O'Gillan

In a quiet watered land, a land of roses,
  Stands Saint Kieran's city fair;
And the warriors of Erin in their famous generations
  Slumber there.

There beneath the dewy hillside sleep the noblest
  Of the clan of Conn,
Each below his stone with name in branching Ogham
  And the sacred knot thereon.

There they laid to rest the seven Kings of Tara,
  There the sons of Cairbrè sleep—
Battle-banners of the Gael, that in Kieran's plain of crosses
  Now their final hosting keep.

And in Clonmacnois they laid the men of Teffia,
  And right many a lord of Breagh;
Deep the sod above Clan Creidè and Clan Conaill,
  Kind in hall and fierce in fray.

Many and many a son of Conn the Hundred-Fighter
  In the red earth lies at rest;
Many a blue eye of Clan Colman the turf covers,
  Many a swan-white breast.

T. W. Rolleston

THE SPELL-STRUCK

She walks as she were moving
  Some mystic dance to tread,
So falls her gliding footstep,
  So leans her listening head;

For once to fairy harping
  She danced upon the hill,

And through her brain and bosom
   The music pulses still.

Her eyes are bright and tearless,
   But wide with yearning pain;
She longs for nothing earthly,
   But O! to hear again

The sound that held her listening
   Upon her moonlit path!
The rippling fairy music
   That filled the lonely rath.

Her lips, that once have tasted
   The fairy banquet's bliss,
Shall glad no mortal lover
   With maiden smile or kiss.

She's dead to all things living
   Since that November Eve;
And when she dies in autumn
   No living thing will grieve.

T. W. Rolleston

WERE YOU ON THE MOUNTAIN?
From the Irish

O, were you on the mountain, or saw you my love?
Or saw you my own one, my queen and my dove?
Or saw you the maiden with the step firm and free?
And say, is she pining in sorrow like me?

I was upon the mountain, and saw there your love,
I saw there your own one, your queen and your dove;
I saw there the maiden with the step firm and free
And she was not pining in sorrow like thee.

Douglas Hyde

MY GRIEF ON THE SEA
From the Irish

My grief on the sea,
   How the waves of it roll!
For they heave between me
   And the love of my soul!

Abandoned, forsaken,
   To grief and to care,
Will the sea ever waken
   Relief from despair?

My grief and my trouble
   Would he and I wear,
In the province of Leinster,
   Or County of Clare?

Were I and my darling—
   O, heart-bitter wound!—
On board of the ship
   For America bound.

On a green bed of rushes
   All last night I lay,
And I flung it abroad
   With the heat of the day.

And my love came behind me—
   He came from the south;
His breast to my bosom,
   His mouth to my mouth.

Douglas Hyde

MY LOVE, O, SHE IS MY LOVE
From the Irish

She casts a spell, O, casts a spell,
    Which haunts me more than I can tell.
    Dearer because she makes me ill,
    Than who would will to make me well.

She is my store, O, she my store,
    Whose grey eye wounded me so sore,
    Who will not place in mine her palm,
    Who will not calm me any more.

She is my pet, O, she my pet,
    Whom I can never more forget;
    Who would not lose by me one moan,
    Nor stone upon my cairn set,

She is my roon, O, she my roon,
    Who tells me nothing, leaves me soon;
    Who would not lose by me one sigh,
    Were death and I within one room.

She is my dear, O, she my dear,
    Who cares not whether I be here.
    Who would not weep when I am dead,
    Who makes me shed the silent tear.

Hard my case, O, hard my case,
    How have I lived so long a space,
    She does not trust me any more,
    But I adore her silent face.

She is my choice, O, she my choice,
    Who never made me to rejoice;
    Who caused my heart to ache so oft,
    Who put no softness in her voice.

Great is my grief, O, great my grief,
   Neglected, scorned beyond belief,
   By her who looks at me askance,
   By her who grants me no relief.

She's my desire, O, my desire,
   More glorious than the bright sun's fire;
   Who more than wind—blown ice more cold,
   Had I the boldness to sit by her.

She it is who stole my heart,
   But left a void and aching smart,
   But if she soften not her eye,
   Then life and I shall surely part.

                              Douglas Hyde

I SHALL NOT DIE FOR THEE
From the Irish

For thee I shall not die,
   Woman high of fame and name;
Foolish men thou mayest slay,
   I and they are not the same.

Why should I expire
   For the fire of any eye,
Slender waist, or swan-like limb,
   Is't for them that I should die?

The round breasts, the fresh skin,
   Cheeks crimson, hair so long and rich;
Indeed, indeed, I shall not die,
   Please God, not I, for any such.

The golden hair, the forehead thin,
   The chaste mien, the gracious ease,

The rounded heel, the languid tone,
 Fools alone find death from these.

Thy sharp wit, thy perfect calm,
 Thy thin palm like foam of sea;
Thy white neck, thy blue eye,
 I shall not die for thee.

Woman, graceful as the swan,
 A wise man did nurture me,
Little palm, white neck, bright eye,
 I shall not die for ye.

     Douglas Hyde

RIDDLES
From the Irish

A great, great house it is,
A golden candlestick it is,
Guess it rightly,
Let it not go by thee.
     Heaven.

There's a garden that I ken,
Full of little gentlemen,
Little caps of blue they wear,
And green ribbons very fair.
     Flax.

He comes to ye amidst the brine
 The butterfly of the sun,
The man of the coat so blue and fine,
 With red thread his shirt is done.
     A Lobster.

You see it come in on the shoulders of men,
Like a thread of the silk it will leave us again.
Turf.

Douglas Hyde

LOUGH BRAY

A little lonely moorland lake,
  Its waters brown and cool and deep—
The cliff, the hills behind it make
  A picture for my heart to keep.

For rock and heather, wave and strand,
  Wore tints I never saw them wear;
The June sunshine was o'er the land,
  Before, 'twas never half so fair!

The amber ripples sang all day,
  And singing spilled their crowns of white
Upon the beach, in thin pale spray
  That streaked the sober sand with light.

The amber ripples sang their song,
  When suddenly from far o'erhead
A lark's pure voice mixed with the throng
  Of lovely things about us spread.

Some flowers were there, so near the brink
  Their shadows in the waves were thrown;
While mosses, green and gray and pink,
  Grew thickly round each smooth dark stone.

And, over all, the summer sky,
  Shut out the town we left behind;
'Twas joy to stand in silence by,
  One bright chain linking mind to mind.

O, little lonely mountain spot!
　　Your place within my heart will be
Apart from all Life's busy lot
　　A true, sweet, solemn memory.

Rose Kavanagh

THE CHILDREN OF LIR

Out upon the sand-dunes thrive the coarse long grasses,
　　Herons standing knee-deep in the brackish pool,
Overhead the sunset fire and flame amasses,
　　And the moon to Eastward rises pale and cool:
Rose and green around her, silver-grey and pearly,
　　Chequered with the black rooks flying home to bed;
For, to wake at daybreak birds must couch them early,
　　And the day's a long one since the dawn was red.

On the chilly lakelet, in that pleasant gloaming,
　　See the sad swans sailing: they shall have no rest:
Never a voice to greet them save the bittern's booming
　　Where the ghostly sallows sway against the West.
'Sister,' saith the grey swan, 'Sister, I am weary,'
　　Turning to the white swan wet, despairing eyes;
'O,' she saith, 'my young one.' 'O,' she saith, 'my dearie,'
　　Casts her wings about him with a storm of cries.

Woe for Lir's sweet children whom their vile stepmother
　　Glamoured with her witch-spells for a thousand years;
Died their father raving—on his throne another—
　　Blind before the end came from his burning tears.
She—the fiends possess her, torture her for ever,
　　Gone is all the glory of the race of Lir;
Gone and long-forgotten like a dream of fever:
　　But the swans remember all the days that were.

Hugh, the black and white swan with the beauteous feathers;
    Fiachra, the black swan with the emerald breast;
Conn, the youngest, dearest, sheltered in all weathers,
    Him his snow-white sister loves the tenderest.
These her mother gave her as she lay a-dying,
    To her faithful keeping, faithful hath she been,
With her wings spread o'er them when the tempest's crying,
    And her songs so hopeful when the sky's serene.

Other swans have nests made 'mid the reeds and rushes,
    Lined with downy feathers where the cygnets sleep
Dreaming, if a bird dreams, till the daylight blushes,
    Then they sail out swiftly on the current deep,
With the proud swan-father, tall, and strong, and stately,
    And the mild swan-mother, grave with household cares,
All well-born and comely, all rejoicing greatly:
    Full of honest pleasure is a life like theirs.

But alas! for my swans, with the human nature,
    Sick with human longings, starved with human ties,
With their hearts all human, cramped in a bird's stature,
    And the human weeping in the bird's soft eyes.
Never shall my swans build nests in some green river,
    Never fly to southward in the autumn grey,
Rear no tender children, love no mates for ever,
    Robbed alike of bird's joys and of man's are they.

Babbled Conn the youngest, 'Sister, I remember
    At my father's palace how I went in silk,
Ate the juicy deer-flesh roasted from the ember,
    Drank from golden goblets my child's draught of milk.
Once I rode a-hunting, laughed to see the hurly,
    Shouted at the ball-play, on the lake did row;
You had for your beauty gauds that shone so rarely':
    'Peace,' saith Finnuola, 'that was long ago.'

'Sister,' saith Fiachra, 'well do I remember
    How the flaming torches lit the banquet hall,
And the fire leaped skyward in the mid-December,
    And amid the rushes slept our staghounds tall.
By our father's right hand you sat shyly gazing,
    Smiling half and sighing, with your eyes aglow,
As the bards sang loudly, all your beauty praising';
    'Peace,' saith Finnuola, 'that was long ago.'

'Sister,' then saith Hugh, 'most do I remember
    One I called my brother, you, earth's goodliest man,
Strong as forest oaks are where the wild vines clamber,
    First at feast or hunting, in the battle's van.
Angus, you were handsome, wise and true and tender,
    Loved by every comrade, feared by every foe:
Low, low lies your beauty, all forgot your splendour':
    'Peace,' saith Finnuola, 'that was long ago.'

Dews are in the clear air, and the roselight paling,
    Over sands and sedges shines the evening star,
And the moon's disk high in heaven is sailing,
    Silvered all the spear-heads of the rushes are—
Housed warm are all things as the night grows colder,
    Water-fowl and sky-fowl dreamless in the nest,
But the swans go drifting, drooping wings and shoulder,
    Cleaving the still waters where the fishes rest.

                              Katharine Tynan Hinkson

ST. FRANCIS TO THE BIRDS

Little sisters, the birds,
    We must praise God, you and I—
    You with songs that fill the sky;
I, with halting words.

All things tell His praise,
  Woods and waters thereof sing,
  Summer, winter, autumn, spring,
And the nights and days.

Yea, and cold and heat,
  And the sun, and stars, and moon,
  Sea with her monotonous tune,
Rain and hail and sleet.

And the winds of heaven,
  And the solemn hills of blue,
  And the brown earth and the dew,
And the thunder even,

And the flowers' sweet breath,—
  All things make one glorious voice;
  Life with fleeting pains and joys
And our brother—Death.

Little flowers of air,
  With your feathers soft and sleek
  And your bright brown eyes and meek,
He hath made you fair.

He hath taught to you
  Skill to weave on tree and thatch
  Nests where happy mothers hatch
Speckled eggs of blue.

And hath children given:
  When the soft heads overbrim
  The brown nests; then thank ye Him
In the clouds of heaven.

Also in your lives,
  Live His laws who loveth you.

Husbands, be ye kind and true;
Be homekeeping wives.

Love not gossiping;
    Stay at home and keep the nest;
    Fly not here and there in quest
Of the newest thing.

Live as brethren live;
    Love be in each heart and mouth;
    Be not envious, be not wroth,
Be not slow to give.

When ye build the nest
    Quarrel not o'er straw or wool;
    He who hath, be bountiful
To the neediest.

Be not puffed or vain
    Of your beauty or your worth,
    Of your children or your birth,
Or the praise you gain.

Eat not greedily:
    Sometimes, for sweet mercy's sake,
    Worm or insect spare to take;
Let it crawl or fly.

See ye sing not near
    To our church on holy day,
    Lest the human-folk should stray
From their prayer to hear.

Now depart in peace,
    In God's name I bless each one;
    May your days be long i' the sun
And your joys increase.

And remember me,
  Your poor brother Francis, who
  Loveth you, and thanketh you
For this courtesy.

Sometimes when ye sing,
  Name my name, that He may take
  Pity for the dear song's sake
On my shortcoming.

                    Katharine Tynan Hinkson

SHEEP AND LAMBS

All in the April morning,
  April airs were abroad;
The sheep with their little lambs
  Passed me by on the road.

The sheep with their little lambs
  Passed me by on the road;
All in the April evening,
  I thought on the Lamb of God.

The lambs were weary, and crying
  With a weak human cry,
I thought on the Lamb of God
  Going meekly to die.

Up in the blue, blue mountains
  Dewy pastures are sweet:
Rest for the little bodies,
  Rest for the little feet.

Rest for the Lamb of God
  Up on the hill-top green,
Only a cross of shame
  Two stark crosses between.

All in the April evening,
    April airs were abroad;
I saw the sheep with their lambs,
    And thought on the Lamb of God.

                Katharine Tynan Hinkson

THE GARDENER SAGE

Here in the garden-bed,
    Hoeing the celery,
Wonders the Lord has made
    Pass ever before me.
I saw the young birds build,
    And swallows come and go,
And summer grow and gild,
    And winter die in snow.

Many a thing I note,
    And store it in my mind;
For all my ragged coat,
    That scarce will stop the wind.
I light my pipe and draw,
    And, leaning on my spade,
I marvel with much awe
    O'er all the Lord hath made.

Now, here's curious thing:
    Upon the first of March,
The crow goes house-building,
    In the elms and in the larch.
And be it shine or snow,
    Though many winds carouse,
That day the artful crow
    Begins to build his house.

But then—the wonder's big!—
  If Sunday fall that day
Nor straw, nor scraw, nor twig,
  Till Monday will he lay.
His black wings to his side,
  He'll drone upon his perch,
Subdued and holy-eyed,
  As though he were at church.

The crow's a gentleman
  Not greatly to my mind,
He'll steal what seeds he can,
  And all you hide he'll find.
Yet though he's bully and sneak,
  To small birds bird of prey—
He counts the days of the week,
  And keeps the Sabbath day.

Katharine Tynan Hinkson

THE DARK MAN

Rose o' the world, she came to my bed
And changed the dreams of my heart and head:
For joy of mine she left grief of hers
And garlanded me with a crown of furze.

Rose o' the world, they go out and in,
And watch me dream and my mother spin:
And they pity the tears on my sleeping face
While my soul's away in a fairy place.

Rose o' the world, they have words galore,
And wide's the swing of my mother's door:
But soft they speak of my darkened eyes,
But what do they know, who are all so wise?

Rose o' the world, the pain you give
Is worth all days that a man may live:
Worth all shy prayers that the colleens say
On the night that darkens the wedding day.

Rose o' the world, what man would wed
When he might dream of your face instead?
Might go to his grave with the blessed pain
Of hungering after your face again?

Rose o' the world, they may talk their fill,
For dreams are good, and my life stands still
While their lives' red ashes the gossips stir,
But my fiddle knows: and I talk to her.

Nora Hopper

THE FAIRY FIDDLER

'Tis I go fiddling, fiddling,
　By weedy ways forlorn:
I make the blackbird's music
　Ere in his breast 'tis born:
The sleeping larks I waken
　Twixt the midnight and the morn.

No man alive has seen me,
　But women hear me play
Sometimes at door or window,
　Fiddling the souls away,—
The child's soul and the colleen's
　Out of the covering clay.

None of my fairy kinsmen
　Make music with me now:
Alone the raths I wander
　Or ride the whitethorn bough;

> But the wild swans they know me,
>> And the horse that draws the plough.

Nora Hopper

OUR THRONES DECAY

I said, my pleasure shall not move;
  It is not fixed in things apart:
Seeking not love—but yet to love—
  I put my trust in mine own heart.

I knew the fountain of the deep
  Wells up with living joy, unfed;
Such joys the lonely heart may keep,
  And love grow rich with love unwed.

Still flows the ancient fount sublime;
  But, ah, for my heart shed tears, shed tears;
Not it, but love, has scorn of time;
  It turns to dust beneath the years.

A. E.

IMMORTALITY

We must pass like smoke or live within the spirit's fire;
For we can no more than smoke unto the flame return
If our thought has changed to dream, our will unto desire,
  As smoke we vanish though the fire may burn.

Lights of infinite pity star the grey dusk of our days:
Surely here is soul: with it we have eternal breath:
In the fire of love we live, or pass by many ways,
  By unnumbered ways of dream to death.

A. E.

THE GREAT BREATH

Its edges foamed with amethyst and rose,
Withers once more the old blue flower of day:
There where the ether like a diamond glows
    Its petals fade away.

A shadowy tumult stirs the dusky air;
Sparkle the delicate dews, the distant snows;
The great deep thrills for through it everywhere
    The breath of Beauty blows.

I saw how all the trembling ages past,
Moulded to her by deep and deeper breath,
Neared to the hour when Beauty breathes her last
    And knows herself in death.

                      A. E.

SUNG ON A BY-WAY

What of all the will to do?
    It has vanished long ago,
For a dream-shaft pierced it through
    From the Unknown Archer's bow.

What of all the soul to think?
    Some one offered it a cup
Filled with a diviner drink,
    And the flame has burned it up.

What of all the hope to climb?
    Only in the self we grope
To the misty end of time:
    Truth has put an end to hope.

What of all the heart to love?
    Sadder than for will or soul,

No light lured it on above;
   Love has found itself the whole.

A. E.

DREAM LOVE

I did not deem it half so sweet
To feel thy gentle hand,
As in a dream thy soul to greet
Across wide leagues of land.

Untouched more near to draw to you
Where, amid radiant skies,
Glimmered thy plumes of iris hue,
My Bird of Paradise.

Let me dream only with my heart,
Love first, and after see:
Know thy diviner counterpart
Before I kneel to thee.

So in thy motions all expressed
Thy angel I may view:
I shall not in thy beauty rest,
But Beauty's ray on you.

A. E.

ILLUSION

What is the love of shadowy lips
That know not what they seek or press,
From whom the lure for ever slips
And fails their phantom tenderness?

The mystery and light of eyes
That near to mine grow dim and cold;

They move afar in ancient skies
Mid flame and mystic darkness rolled.

O beauty, as thy heart o'erflows
In tender yielding unto me,
A vast desire awakes and grows
Unto forgetfulness of thee.

A. E.

JANUS

Image of beauty, when I gaze on thee,
Trembling I waken to a mystery,
How through one door we go to life or death
By spirit kindled or the sensual breath.

Image of beauty, when my way I go;
No single joy or sorrow do I know:
Elate for freedom leaps the starry power,
The life which passes mourns its wasted hour.

And, ah, to think how thin the veil that lies
Between the pain of hell and paradise!
Where the cool grass my aching head embowers
God sings the lovely carol of the flowers.

A. E.

CONNLA'S WELL

A cabin on the mountain side hid in a grassy nook,
With door and windows open wide where friendly stars may
    look;
The rabbit shy can patter in; the winds may enter free
Who throng around the mountain throne in living ecstasy.

And when the sun sets dimmed in eve and purple fills the air,
I think the sacred hazel tree is dropping berries there

From starry fruitage waved aloft where Connla's well o'erflows;
For sure the immortal waters run through every wind that
   blows.

I think when night towers up aloft and shakes the trembling
   dew,
How every high and lonely thought that thrills my spirit through
Is but a shining berry dropped down through the purple air,
And from the magic tree of life the fruit falls everywhere.

A. E.

NAMES

No temple crowned the shaggy capes,
   No safety soothed the kind,
The clouds unfabled shifted shapes,
   And nameless roamed the wind.

The stars, the circling heights of heaven,
   The mountains bright with snows
Looked down, and sadly man at even
   Lay down and sad he rose.

Till ages brought the hour again,
   When fell a windless morn,
And, child of agonistic pain
   And bliss, the Word was born.

Which grew from all it gazed upon,
   And spread thro' soil and sphere,
And shrunk the whole into the one,
   And fetched the farthest here.

High is the summer's night, but deep
   The hidden mind unfolds:
Within it does an image sleep
   Of all that it beholds.

Alas! when man with busy brow,
    His conquering names hath set
To planet, plant, and worm, who now
    Will teach us to forget?

What poet now, when wisdoms fail,
    Another theme shall dare—
The Nameless, and remove the veil
    Which hides it everywhere?

                    John Eglinton

THAT

What is that beyond thy life,
And beyond all life around,
Which, when thy quick brain is still,
Nods to thee from the stars?
Lo, it says, thou hast found
Me, the lonely, lonely one.

                    Charles Weekes

THINK

Think, the ragged turf-boy urges
    O'er the dusty road his asses;
Think, on sea-shore far the lonely
    Heron wings along the sand;

Think, in woodland under oak-boughs
    Now the streaming sunbeam passes;
And bethink thee thou art servant
    To the same all-moving hand.

                    Charles Weekes

TE MARTYRUM CANDIDATUS

Ah, see the fair chivalry come, the companions of Christ!
White Horsemen, who ride on white horses, the Knights of
   God!
They, for their Lord and their Lover who sacrificed
All, save the sweetness of treading, where he first trod!

These through the darkness of death, the dominion of night,
Swept, and they woke in white places at morning tide:
They saw with their eyes, and sang for joy of the sight,
They saw with their eyes the Eyes of the Crucified.

Now, whithersoever He goeth, with Him they go:
White Horsemen, who ride on white horses, oh fair to see!
They ride, where the Rivers of Paradise flash and flow,
White Horsemen, with Christ their Captain: for ever He!

Lionel Johnson

THE CHURCH OF A DREAM

Sadly the dead leaves rustle in the whistling wind,
Around the weather-worn gray church, low down the vale:
The Saints in golden vesture shake before the gale;
The glorious windows shake, where still they dwell enshrined;
Old Saints, by long dead, shrivelled hands, long since designed:
There still, although the world autumnal be, and pale,
Still in their golden vesture the old saints prevail;
Alone with Christ, desolate else, left by mankind.
Only one ancient Priest offers the sacrifice,
Murmuring holy Latin immemorial:
Swaying with tremulous hands the old censer full of spice,
In gray, sweet incense clouds; blue, sweet clouds mystical:
To him, in place of men, for he is old, suffice
Melancholy remembrances and vesperal.

Lionel Johnson

WAYS OF WAR

A terrible and splendid trust
   Heartens the host of Inisfail:
Their dream is of the swift sword-thrust,
   A lightning glory of the Gael.

Croagh Patrick is the place of prayers,
   And Tara the assembling place:
But each sweet wind of Ireland bears
   The trump of battle on its race.

From Dursey Isle to Donegal,
   From Howth to Achill, the glad noise
Rings: and the heirs of glory fall,
   Or victory crowns their fighting joys.

A dream! a dream! an ancient dream!
   Yet, ere peace come to Inisfail,
Some weapons on some field must gleam,
   Some burning glory fire the Gael.

That field may lie beneath the sun,
   Fair for the treading of an host:
That field in realms of thought be won,
   And armed minds do their uttermost:

Some way, to faithful Inisfail,
   Shall come the majesty and awe
Of martial truth, that must prevail,
   To lay on all the eternal law.

                   Lionel Johnson

THE RED WIND

Red Wind from out the East:
   Red wind of blight and blood!

Ah, when wilt thou have ceased.
 Thy bitter, stormy flood?

Red Wind from over sea,
 Scourging our holy land!
What angel loosened thee
 Out of his iron hand?

Red Wind! whose word of might
 Winged thee with wings of flame?
O fire of mournful night!
 What is thy Master's name?

Red Wind! who bade thee burn,
 Branding our hearts? Who bade
Thee on and never turn,
 Till waste our souls were laid?

Red Wind! from out the West
 Pour Winds of Paradise:
Winds of eternal rest,
 That weary souls entice.

Wind of the East! Red Wind!
 Thou scorchest the soft breath
Of Paradise the kind:
 Red Wind of burning death!

O Red Wind! hear God's voice:
 Hear thou, and fall, and cease.
Let Inisfail rejoice
 In her Hesperian peace.

Lionel Johnson

CELTIC SPEECH

Never forgetful silence fall on thee,
    Nor younger voices overtake thee,
Nor echoes from thine ancient hills forsake thee,
    Old music heard by Mona of the sea:
And where with moving melodies there break thee,
    Pastoral Conway, venerable Dee.

Like music lives, nor may that music die,
    Still in the far, fair Gaelic places:
The speech, so wistful with its kindly graces,
    Holy Croagh Patrick knows, and holy Hy:
The speech, that wakes the soul in withered faces,
    And wakes remembrance of great things gone by.

Like music by the desolate Land's End,
    Mournful forgetfulness hath broken:
No more words kindred to the winds are spoken,
    Where upon iron cliffs whole seas expend
That strength, whereof the unalterable token
    Remains wild music, even to the world's end.

                                        Lionel Johnson

TO MORFYDD

A voice on the winds,
A voice on the waters,
        Wanders and cries:

O! what are the winds?
And what are the waters?
        Mine are your eyes.

Western the winds are,
And western the waters,
        Where the light lies:

O! what are the winds?
And what are the waters?
     Mine are your eyes.

Cold, cold, grow the winds,
And dark grow the waters,
     Where the sun dies:

O! what are the winds?
And what are the waters?
     Mine are your eyes.

And down the night winds,
And down the night waters
     The music flies:

O! what are the winds?
And what are the waters?
Cold be the winds,
And wild be the waters,
     So mine be your eyes.

Lionel Johnson

CAN DOOV DEELISH

Can doov deelish, beside the sea
I stand and stretch my hands to thee
     Across the world.
The riderless horses race to shore
With thundering hoofs and shuddering, hoar,
     Blown manes uncurled.

Can doov deelish, I cry to thee
Beyond the world, beneath the sea,
     Thou being dead.

Where hast thou hidden from the beat
Of crushing hoofs and tearing feet
        Thy dear black head?

God bless the woman, whoever she be,
From the tossing waves will recover thee
        And lashing wind.

Who will take thee out of the wind and storm,
Dry thy wet face on her bosom warm
        And lips so kind?

I not to know. It is hard to pray,
But I shall for this woman from day to day,
        'Comfort my dead,
The sport of the winds and the play of the sea.'
I loved thee too well for this thing to be,
        O dear black head!
                Dora Sigerson

Anonymous

SHULE AROON

I would I were on yonder hill,
'Tis there I'd sit and cry my fill,
And every tear would turn a mill,
Is go de tu mo vuirnin slàn.
Shule, shule, shule aroon,
Shule go succir, agus shule go cuin,
Shule go den durrus agus eligh lum,
Is go de tu mo vuirnin slàn.

I'll sell my rock, I'll sell my reel,
I'll sell my only spinning-wheel,
To buy for my love a sword of steel,
Is go de tu mo vuirnin slàn.

Chorus.

I'll dye my petticoats, I'll dye them red,
And around the world I'll beg my bread,
Until my parents shall wish me dead,
Is go de tu mo vuirnin slàn.

Chorus.

I wish, I wish, I wish in vain,
I wish I had my heart again,
And vainly think I'd not complain,
Is go de tu mo vuirnin slàn.

Chorus.

But now my love has gone to France,
To try his fortune to advance;
If he e'er come back 'tis but a chance,
Is go de tu mo vuirnin slàn.

Chorus.

THE SHAN VAN VOCHT

O! the French are on the sea,
  Says the *shan van vocht*;
The French are on the sea,
  Says the *shan van vocht*;
O! the French are in the bay,
They'll be here without delay,
And the Orange will decay,
  Says the *shan van vocht*.

Chorus.

  O! the French are in the bay,
  They'll be here by break of day,
  And the Orange will decay,
    Says the *shan van vocht*.

And their camp it shall be where?
  Says the *shan van vocht*;
Their camp it shall be where?
  Says the *shan van vocht*;
On the Currach of Kildare,
The boys they will be there,
With their pikes in good repair,
  Says the *shan van vocht*.

  To the Currach of Kildare
  The boys they will repair,
  And Lord Edward will be there,
    Says the *shan van vocht*.

Then what will the yeomen do?
  Says the *shan van vocht*;
What will the yeomen do?
  Says the *shan van vocht*;

What *should* the yeomen do
But throw off the red and blue,
And swear that they'll be true
   To the *shan van vocht?*

> What *should* the yeomen do
> But throw off the red and blue,
> And swear that they'll be true
>   To the *shan van vocht?*

And what colour will they wear?
   Says the *shan van vocht;*
What colour will they wear?
   Says the *shan van vocht;*
What colour should be seen
Where our fathers' homes have been,
But our own immortal Green?
   Says the *shan van vocht.*

> What colour should be seen
> Where our fathers' homes have been,
> But our own immortal Green?
>   Says the *shan van vocht.*

And will Ireland then be free?
   Says the *shan van vocht;*
Will Ireland then be free?
   Says the *shan van vocht;*
Yes! Ireland SHALL be free,
From the centre to the sea;
Then hurra! for Liberty!
   Says the *shan van vocht.*

> Yes! Ireland SHALL be free,
> From the centre to the sea;
> Then hurra! for Liberty!
>   Says the *shan van vocht.*

THE WEARING OF THE GREEN

O Paddy dear, and did you hear the news that's going round?
The shamrock is forbid by law to grow on Irish ground;
St. Patrick's day no more we'll keep, his colours can't be seen,
For there's a bloody law agin the wearing of the green.
I met with Napper Tandy, and he took me by the hand,
And he said, 'How's poor old Ireland, and how does she stand?'
She's the most distressful country that ever yet was seen,
They are hanging men and women for the wearing of the green.

Then if the colour we must wear be England's cruel red,
Let it remind us of the blood that Ireland has shed.
You may take the shamrock from your hat and cast it on the sod,
But 'twill take root and flourish there, though under foot 'tis
    trod.
When law can stop the blades of grass from growing as they
    grow,
And when the leaves in summer-time their verdure dare not
    show,
Then I will change the colour that I wear in my caubeen,
But 'till that day, please God, I'll stick to wearing of the green.

THE RAKES OF MALLOW

Beauing, belleing, dancing, drinking,
Breaking windows, damning, sinking,
Ever raking, never thinking,
                Live the rakes of Mallow.

Spending faster than it comes,
Beating waiters, bailiffs, duns,
Bacchus's true-begotten sons,
                Live the rakes of Mallow.

One time nought but claret drinking,
Then like politicians thinking
To raise the sinking funds when sinking,
Live the rakes of Mallow.

When at home with dadda dying,
Still for Mallow water crying;
But where there's good claret plying,
Live the rakes of Mallow.

Living short, but merry lives;
Going where the devil drives;
Having sweethearts, but no wives,
Live the rakes of Mallow.

Racking tenants, stewards teasing,
Swiftly spending, slowly raising,
Wishing to spend all their days in
Raking as at Mallow.

Then to end this raking life
They get sober, take a wife,
Ever after live in strife,
And wish again for Mallow.

JOHNNY, I HARDLY KNEW YE
Street ballad

While going the road to sweet Athy,
Hurroo! hurroo!
While going the road to sweet Athy,
Hurroo! hurroo!
While going the road to sweet Athy,
A stick in my hand and a drop in my eye,
A doleful damsel I heard cry:—
'Och, Johnny, I hardly knew ye!

With drums and guns and guns and drums
    The enemy nearly slew ye,
    My darling dear, you look so queer,
Och, Johnny, I hardly knew ye!

'Where are your eyes that looked so mild?
    Hurroo! hurroo!
Where are your eyes that looked so mild?
    Hurroo! hurroo!
Where are your eyes that looked so mild,
When my poor heart you first beguiled?
Why did you run from me and the child?
    Och, Johnny, I hardly knew ye!
With drums, etc.

'Where are the legs with which you run?
    Hurroo! hurroo!
Where are the legs with which you run?
    Hurroo! hurroo!
Where are the legs with which you run,
When you went to carry a gun?—
Indeed, your dancing days are done!
    Och, Johnny, I hardly knew ye
With drums, etc.

'It grieved my heart to see you sail,
    Hurroo! hurroo!
It grieved my heart to see you sail,
    Hurroo! hurroo!
Though from my heart you took leg bail,—
Like a cod you're doubled up head and tail.
    Och, Johnny, I hardly knew ye!
With drums, etc.

'You haven't an arm and you haven't a leg,
    Hurroo! hurroo!

You haven't an arm and you haven't a leg,
      Hurroo! hurroo!
You haven't an arm and you haven't a leg,
You're an eyeless, noseless, chickenless egg;
You'll have to be put in a bowl to beg:
      Och, Johnny, I hardly knew ye!
With drums, etc.

'I'm happy for to see you home,
      Hurroo! hurroo!
I'm happy for to see you home,
      Hurroo! hurroo!

I'm happy for to see you home,
All from the island of Sulloon,
So low in flesh, so high in bone,
      Och, Johnny, I hardly knew ye!
With drums, etc.

'But sad as it is to see you so,
      Hurroo! hurroo!
But sad as it is to see you so,
      Hurroo! hurroo!
But sad as it is to see you so,
And to think of you now as an object of woe,
Your Peggy'll still keep ye on as her beau;
      Och, Johnny, I hardly knew ye!

'With drums and guns and guns and drums,
    The enemy nearly slew ye,
    My darling dear, you look so queer,
Och, Johnny, I hardly knew ye!'

KITTY OF COLERAINE

As beautiful Kitty one morning was tripping
    With a pitcher of milk from the fair of Coleraine,
When she saw me she stumbled, the pitcher down tumbled,
    And all the sweet buttermilk watered the plain.
O! what shall I do now? 'Twas looking at you, now;
    Sure, sure, such a pitcher I'll ne'er meet again;
'Twas the pride of my dairy! O Barney O'Cleary,
    You're sent as a plague to the girls of Coleraine!

I sat down beside her, and gently did chide her,
    That such a misfortune should give her such pain;
A kiss then I gave her, and ere I did leave her,
    She vowed for such pleasure she'd break it again.
'Twas haymaking season—I can't tell the reason—
    Misfortunes will never come single 'tis plain;
For very soon after poor Kitty's disaster
    The devil a pitcher was whole in Coleraine.

LAMENT OF MORIAN SHEHONE FOR MISS MARY BOURKE
From an Irish keen

'There's darkness in thy dwelling-place, and silence reigns
    above,
And Mary's voice is heard no more, like the soft voice of love.
Yes! thou art gone, my Mary dear! and Morian Shehone
Is left to sing his song of woe, and wail for thee alone.
O! snow-white were thy virtues—the beautiful, the young,
The old with pleasure bent to hear the music of thy tongue:
The young with rapture gazed on thee, and their hearts in love
    were bound,
For thou wast brighter than the sun that sheds its light around.

My soul is dark, O Mary dear! thy sun of beauty's set;
The sorrowful are dumb for thee—the grieved their tears forget;
And I am left to pour my woe above thy grave alone;
For dear wert thou to the fond heart of Morian Shehone
Fast-flowing tears above the grave of the rich man are shed,
But they are dried when the cold stone shuts in his narrow bed;
Not so with my heart's faithful love—the dark grave cannot hide
From Morian's eyes thy form of grace, of loveliness, and pride.
Thou didst not fall like the sere leaf, when autumn's chill winds
    blow—
'Twas a tempest and a storm-blast that has laid my Mary low.
Hadst thou not friends that loved thee well? hadst thou not
    garments rare?
Wast thou not happy, Mary? wast thou not young and fair?
Then why should the dread spoiler come, my heart's peace to
    destroy,
Or the grim tyrant tear from me my all of earthly joy?
O! am I left to pour my woes above thy grave alone?
Thou idol of the faithful heart of Morian Shehone!
Sweet were thy looks and sweet thy smiles, and kind wast thou to
    all;
The withering scowl of envy on thy fortunes dared not fall;
For thee thy friends lament and mourn, and never cease to
    weep—
O! that their lamentations could awake thee from thy sleep!
O! that thy peerless form again could meet my loving clasp!
O! that the cold damp hand of Death could loose his iron grasp!
Yet, when the valley's daughters meet beneath the tall elm tree,
And talk of Mary as a dream that never more shall be,
Then may thy spirit float around, like music in the air,
And pour upon their virgin souls a blessing and a prayer.
O! am I left to pour my wail above thy grave alone?'
Then sinks in silence the lament of Morian Shehone!

THE GERALDINE'S DAUGHTER

Speak low!—speak low—the banshee is crying;
Hark! hark to the echo!—she's dying! 'she's dying.'
What shadow flits dark'ning the face of the water?
'Tis the swan of the lake—'tis *the Geraldine's Daughter.*

Hush, hush! have you heard what the banshee said?
O! list to the echo! she's dead! 'she's dead!'
No shadow now dims the face of the water;
Gone, gone is the wraith of *the Geraldine's Daughter.*

The step of you train is heavy and slow,
There's wringing of hands, there's breathing of woe;
What melody rolls over mountain and water?
'Tis the funeral chant of *the Geraldine's Daughter.*

The requiem sounds like the plaintive moan
Which the wind makes over the sepulchre's stone;
'O, why did she die? our hearts' blood had bought her!
O, why did she die, *the Geraldine's Daughter?*'

The thistle-beard floats—the wild roses wave
With the blast that sweeps over the newly-made grave;
The stars dimly twinkle, and hoarse falls the water,
While night-birds are wailing *the Geraldine's Daughter.*

BY MEMORY INSPIRED
Street ballad

By Memory inspired,
And love of country fired,
The deeds of Men I love to dwell upon;
And the patriotic glow
Of my spirit must bestow

A tribute to O'Connell that is gone, boys, gone!
Here's a memory to the friends that are gone.

In October 'Ninety-seven—
May his soul find rest in Heaven—
William Orr to execution was led on:
The jury, drunk, agreed
That Irish was his creed;
For perjury and threats drove them on, boys, on:
Here's the memory of John Mitchell that is gone

In 'Ninety-Eight—the month July—
The informer's pay was high;
When Reynolds gave the gallows brave MacCann;
But MacCann was Reynolds' first—
One could not allay his thirst;
So he brought up Bond and Byrne, that are gone, boys, gone.
Here's the memory of the friends that are gone!

We saw a nation's tears
Shed for John and Henry Shears;
Betrayed by Judas, Captain Armstrong;
We may forgive, but yet
We never can forget
The poisoning of Maguire that is gone, boys, gone—
Our high Star and true Apostle that is gone!

How did Lord Edward die?
Like a man, without a sigh;
But he left his handiwork on Major Swan!
But Sirr, with steel-clad breast,
And coward heart at best,
Left us cause to mourn Lord Edward that is gone, boys, gone:
Here's the memory of our friends that are gone!

September, Eighteen-three,
Closed this cruel history,

When Emmett's blood the scaffold flowed upon
    O, had their spirits been wise,
    They might then realize
Their freedom—but we drink to Mitchell that is gone, boys, gone:
Here's the memory of the friends that are gone!

A FOLK VERSE

When you were an acorn on the tree top,
    Then was I an eagle cock;
Now that you are a withered old block,
    Still am I an eagle cock.

NOTES

Page xxii, lines 9 to 13.   A well-known poet of the Fenian times has made the curious boast—'Talking of work—since Sunday, two cols. Notes, two cols. London gossip, and a leader one col., and one col. of verse for the *Nation*. For *Catholic Opinion*, two pages of notes and a leader. For *Illustrated Magazine*, three poems and a five-col. story.'

Page 1.   'The deserted village' is Lissoy, near Ballymahon, and Sir Walter Scott tells of a hawthorn there which has been cut up into toothpicks by Goldsmith enthusiasts; but the feeling and atmosphere of the poem are unmistakably English.

Pages 5–6.   Some verses in 'The Epicurean' were put into French by Théophile Gautier for the French translation, and back again into English by Mr. Robert Bridges. If any Irish reader who thinks Moore a great poet, will compare his verses with the results of this double distillation, and notice the gradual disappearance of their vague rhythms and loose phrases, he will be the less angry with the introduction to this book. Moore wrote as follows—

> You, who would try
>   You terrible track,
> To live or to die,
>   But ne'er to turn back.

You, who aspire
   To be purified there,
By the terror of fire,
   Of water, and air,—

If danger, and pain,
   And death you despise,
On—for again
   Into light you shall rise:

Rise into light
   With the secret divine,
Now shrouded from sight
   By a veil of the shrine.

These lines are certainly less amazing than the scrannel piping of his usual anapæsts; but few will hold them to be 'of their own arduous fullness reverent'! Théophile Gautier sets them to his instrument in this fashion,

Vous qui voulez courir
La terrible carrière,
Il faut vivre ou mourir,
Sans regard en arrière:

Vous qui voulez tenter
L'onde, l'air, et la flamme,
Terreurs à surmonter
Pour épurer votre âme,

Si, méprisant la mort,
Votre foi reste entière,
En avant!—le cœur fort
Reverra la lumière.

Et lira sur l'autel
Le mot du grand mystère,
Qu'au profane mortel
Dérobe un voile austère.

Then comes Mr. Robert Bridges, and lifts them into the rapture and precision of poetry—

O youth whose hope is high,
Who dost to truth aspire,
Whether thou live or die,
O look not back nor tire.

Thou that art bold to fly
Through tempest, flood, and fire,
Nor dost not shrink to try
Thy heart in torments dire:

If thou canst Death defy,
If thy faith is entire,
Press onward, for thine eye
Shall see thy heart's desire.

Beauty and love are nigh,
And with their deathless quire—
Soon shall thine eager cry
Be numbered and expire.

Page 18. 'Dark Rosaleen' is one of the old names of Ireland. Mangan's translation is very free; as a rule when he tried to translate literally, as in 'The Munster Bards,' all glimmer of inspiration left him.

Page 22, line 2. 'This passage is not exactly a blunder, though at first it may seem one: the poet supposes the grave itself transferred to Ireland, and he naturally includes in the transference the whole of the immediate locality about the grave' (Mangan note).

Page 31, line 10. The two Meaths once formed a distinct province.

Page 36, line 5. This poem is an account of Mangan's own life, and is, I think, redeemed out of rhetoric by its intensity. The following poem, 'Siberia,' describes, perhaps, his own life under a symbol.

Page 39. Hy Brasail, or Teer-Nan-Oge, is the island of the blessed, the paradise of ancient Ireland. It is still thought to be seen from time to time glimmering far off.

Page 40. *Mo Craoibhin Cno* means my cluster of nuts, and is pronounced *Mo Chreevin Knō.*

Page 41. Mr. O'Keefe has sent the writer a Gaelic version of this poem, possibly by Walsh himself. A correspondent of his got it from an old peasant who had not a word of English. A well-known Gaelic scholar pronounces it a translation, and not the original of the present poem. *Mairgréad ni Chealleadh* is pronounced *Mairgréd nei Kealley.* The *Ceanabhan,* pronounced *Kanovan*, is the bog cotton, and the *Monadan* is a plant with a red berry found on marshy mountains.

Page 45. *A cuisle geal mo chroidhe*, pronounced *A cushla gal mo chre*, means 'bright pulse of my heart.'

Page 48. Sir Samuel Ferguson introduces the poem as follows:

Several Welsh families, associates in the invasion of Strongbow, settled in the West of Ireland. Of these, the principal, whose names have been preserved by the Irish antiquarians, were the Walshes, Joyces, Heils (*a quibus* MacHale), Lawlesses, Tolmyns, Lynotts, and Barretts, which last draw their pedigree from Walynes, son of Guyndally, the *Ard Maor*, or High Steward of the Lordship of Camelot, and had their chief seats in the territory of the two Bacs, in the barony of Tirawley, and county of Mayo. *Clochan-na-n'all*, i.e. 'The Blind Men's Stepping-stones,' are still pointed out on the Duvowen river, about four miles north of Crossmolina, in the townland of Garranard; and *Tubber-na-Scorney*, or 'Scrags Well,' in the opposite townland of Carns, in the same barony. For a curious *terrier* or applotment of the Mac William's revenue, as acquired under the circumstances stated in the legend preserved by Mac Firbis, see Dr. O'Donovan's highly-learned and interesting 'Genealogies, &c. of Hy. Fiachrach,' in the publications of the *Irish Archæological Society*—a great monument of antiquarian and topographical erudition.

Page 59, line 17. 'William Conquer' was William Fitzadelm De Burgh, the Conqueror of Connaught.

Page 60, line 5. Sir Samuel Ferguson introduces the poem as follows:—

Aideen, daughter of Angus of Ben-Edar (now the Hill of Howth), died of grief for the loss of her husband, Oscar, son of Ossian, who was slain at the battle of Gavra (*Gowra*, near Tara in Meath), A.D. 284. Oscar was entombed in the rath or earthen fortress that occupied part of the field of battle, the rest of the slain being cast in a pit outside. Aideen is said to have been buried on Howth, near the mansion of her father, and poetical tradition represents the Fenian heroes as present at her obsequies. The Cromlech in Howth Park has been supposed to be her sepulchre. It stands under the summits from which the poet Atharne is said to have launched his invectives against the people of Leinster, until, by the blighting effect of his satires, they were compelled to make him atonement for the death of his son.

Page 66. 'There was then no man in the host of Ulster that could be found who would put the sons of Usnach to death, so loved were they of the people and nobles. But in the house of Conor was one called Mainé

Rough Hand, son of the king of Lochlen, and Naesi had slain his father and two brothers, and he undertook to be their executioners. So the sons of Usnach were then slain, and the men of Ulster, when they beheld their death, sent forth their heavy shouts of sorrow and lamentation. Then Deirdre fell down beside their bodies wailing and weeping, and she tore her hair and garments and bestowed kisses on their lifeless lips and bitterly bemoaned them. And a grave was opened for them, and Deirdre, standing by it, with her hair dishevelled and shedding tears abundantly, chanted their funeral song.' (*Hibernian Nights' Entertainment.*)

Page 68. *Uileacan Dubh O'*, pronounced *Uileacaun Doov O*, is a phrase of lamentation.

Page 71, line 25. 'Anna Grace' is the heroine of another ballad by Ferguson. She also was stolen by the Fairies.

Page 74, and line 8. Thomas Davis had an Irish father and a Welsh mother, and Emily Brontë an Irish father and a Cornish mother, and there seems no reason for including the first and excluding the second. I find, perhaps fancifully, an Irish vehemence in 'Remembrance.' Several of the Irish poets have been of mixed Irish-Celtic and British-Celtic blood. William Blake has been recently claimed as of Irish descent, upon the evidence of Dr. Carter Blake; and if, in the course of years, that claim becomes generally accepted, he should be included also in Irish anthologies.

Page 78, line 23. 'The little Black Rose' is but another form of 'Dark Rosaleen,' and has a like significance. 'The Silk of the Kine' is also an old name for Ireland.

Page 90. *Maire Bhan Astór* is pronounced *Mauria vaun a-stór*, and means 'Fair Mary, my treasure.'

Page 92. *Mo bhuachaill*, pronounced *mo Vohil*, means 'my boy.'

Page 112. The Goban Saor, the mason Goban, is a familiar personage in Irish folk-lore, and the reputed builder of the round towers.

Page 123. *Slainté*, ['your] health.'

Page 135. 'And their step-mother, being jealous of their father's great love for them, cast upon the king's children, by sorcery, the shape of swans, and bade them go roaming, even till Patrick's mass-bell should sound in Erin; but no farther in time than that did her power extend.'—*The Fate of the Children of Lir.*

Page 145. The wind was one of the deities of the Pagan Irish. 'The murmuring of the Red Wind from the East,' says an old poem, 'is heard in its course by the strong as well as the weak; it is the wind that wastes the bottom of the trees, and injurious to man is that red wind.'

Page 154. *Can Doov Deelish* means 'dear black head.'

Page 159. The chorus is pronounced *Shoo-il, shoo-il, shoo-il, a rooin, Shoo-il go socair, ogus shoo-il go kiune, Shoo-il go den durrus ogus euli liom, Iss go de too, mo vourneen, slaun*, and means—

> 'Move, move, move, O treasure,
> Move quietly and move gently,
> Move to the door, and fly with me,
> And mayest thou go, my darling, safe!'

Page 160.   *Shan van vocht*, meaning 'little old woman,' is a name for Ireland.

Page 162.   This is not the most ancient form of the ballad, but it is the form into which it was recast by Boucicault, and which has long taken the place of all others.

Page 162, line 18.   'Sinking,' violent swearing.

THE END